TALKING ABOUT

GENESIS

A Resource Guide

TALKING ABOUT

GENESIS

A Resource Guide

PUBLIC AFFAIRS TELEVISION

MAIN
STREET
BOOKS

DOUBLEDAY
NEW YORK   LONDON   TORONTO   SYDNEY   AUCKLAND

A MAIN STREET BOOK
PUBLISHED BY DOUBLEDAY
a division of Bantam Doubleday Dell Publishing Group, Inc.
1540 Broadway, New York, New York 10036

MAIN STREET BOOKS, DOUBLEDAY, and the portrayal of a building
with a tree are trademarks of Doubleday,
a division of Bantam Doubleday Dell Publishing Group, Inc.

Book design by Stanley S. Drate/Folio Graphics Co., Inc.

Biblical excerpts in Chapters 3, 4, and 10 from *The Five Books of Moses*,
by Everett Fox, copyright © 1983, 1986, 1990, 1995 by Schocken
Books, Inc. Reprinted by permission of Schocken Books, published by
Pantheon Books, a division of Random House, Inc.

"Raising Cain" from *Friedman's Fables* by Edwin H. Friedman,
copyright © 1990 by Guilford Press.
Reprinted by permission of Guilford Press.

"The Drowning of the World" by Jack Miles,
copyright © 1996 by Jack Miles.

Library of Congress Cataloging-in-Publication Data

Talking about Genesis : a resource guide / Public Affairs Television.
   — 1st Main Street Books ed.
      p.   cm.
   Includes bibliographical references.
   1. Bible. O.T. Genesis—Criticism, interpretation, etc.
   I. Public Affairs Television (Firm)
   BS1235.2.T35   1996
222'.11'007—dc20   96-9715
                                                              CIP

ISBN 0-385-48580-8

10   9   8   7   6   5   4   3   2

First Main Street Books Edition

CONTENTS

6   A FAMILY AFFAIR

7   THE TEST

8   BLESSED DECEPTION

SECTION III
RESOURCES

SECTION I

BEGINNINGS

INTRODUCTION
by Bill Moyers

Adam and Eve in the Garden of Eden . . . Noah and the Flood . . . God's call to Abraham . . . Jacob wrestling with the angel . . . Joseph in exile in Egypt. The stories found in the Book of Genesis captured our ancestors' imaginations more than three thousand years ago—and they hold us today. What explains their power and endurance?

For one thing, to millions of people they are more than stories, they are sacred texts, sanctified over time by so many communities of faith that they resonate with a power and knowledge beyond our own.

They also challenge. These stories do not all have happy endings. They offer no easy answers to hard questions. They can leave us puzzled, forcing us to confront our own quandaries without pat solutions. Reading the story of Noah and the Flood, I am haunted by the ordeal of the survivor. I find Noah after the Flood both mystifying and troubling: God had spared him because he was a man "righteous in his generation," but he hardly behaves the way we'd expect a model of righteousness to behave. His story is full of contradictions and divine mystery—just like most of the stories in Genesis, just like our own.

But these stories also speak to us today because they are so starkly human. The people in Genesis rage at one another and at God; they struggle with temptation; they are jealous, grief-stricken, patient, conniving, loving, and hateful. And the dilemmas they face are ours: sibling rivalry and family violence; infertility and surrogate parenting; parents who play favorites; husbands who fail their wives; parents who grow old and frail and children who are coming of age. Because their emotions and struggles are so real, the people of Genesis come to life in every generation, and their stories live on.

Furthermore, because the action can spill across generations, the resulting space in the stories gives us room to read ourselves into them. We begin to connect to past generations and to better understand our lives and our relationships, to one another and to the Creator.

Of course, our very different readings of the Bible have too often set us at odds with one another, but the potential is still there, as we discovered in taping our PBS series, for the stories of Genesis to provide us a starting place in a common discussion about life on this planet. We asked Muslims to participate in our discussions because, although this is not their book, it seemed important for Christians, Jews, and Muslims to address ways that our stories, which started in the same place with Abraham, went in very different directions. The stories of Genesis recall that common origin, summon from us a more powerful empathy, and enable us—even late in life—to find new paths to wisdom despite our differences.

It has now been more than five years since I had the chance to sit in on the extraordinary conversation that reconfirmed for me the power of the Genesis stories to draw people together and inspired me to do this series. Although I had studied the Bible in seminary and re-read it over the years, I have never seen anything like Rabbi Burton Visotzky's Genesis discussion group at the Jewish Theological Seminary of America in New York City. The evening I visited, I watched in amazement as a group of novelists, poets, screenwriters, literary critics, and Bible scholars—Christians and Jews—engaged in one of the liveliest, most provocative discussions I have ever heard on the Bible.

I had expected the Genesis group to be passionate about the Bible and the power of ideas—and they were. But I had not imagined that I would actually be able to see one person learn from another or that I would find so many smart, funny people—believers and nonbelievers alike—who were willing to challenge conventional opinion and one another, suggesting new ways to look at the text. I left the Seminary that night committed to trying to capture on camera what I had experienced firsthand, so that a far larger audience could experience it, too.

There are many reasons why I wanted to make this series. I hoped that it would serve to introduce (or reintroduce) many people to these stories and the role they have played in shaping our culture and our consciousness. I hoped that by watching a diverse group of interesting people wrestle with their own beliefs, with one another, and with some of the critical issues we face today, the rest of us might be moved to engage in the same struggle. I hoped that by showing people of different backgrounds and beliefs learning from one another, the series would inspire us to listen to other people's stories and try to see the world through different eyes, to reach for what novelist Alice Walker has called "the unifying theme through immense diversity . . . of growth, of search, of looking, that enlarges the private and the public world."

And, frankly, I hoped to demonstrate that a different kind of religious discourse is taking place in this country beyond the politicized rhetoric about God that has made it so difficult for us to hear one another. Yes, believers are also citizens who should take sides on issues important to their families, communities, and consciences. But an arrogance is abroad in the land about who has a lock on God, a partisan spirit permeates the dialogue, and we are talking at, not with, each other. In one of her poems Kathleen Norris acknowledges that "we are God's chosen now," but goes on to pray "God help us" because of it. The call is to responsibility, not privilege, to humility instead of pride. This spirit prevailed in the discussions for our series, as participants of different faiths listened closely and respectfully to others and even bowed occasionally to the democratic necessity of deferring to the knowledge and opinions of other people.

A television program can introduce ideas, but only people can make things happen. What can you do? I hope you will form your own Genesis group. You can ask family, friends, coworkers, or members of your church, synagogue, or mosque to join you. There is no "right way" to do it—these stories may be old and familiar or brand-new to you; you may have had years of religious education or none at all; you may come as a believer or as a doubter. But come for the adventure. Having lived the experience for the past year, I can tell you that I don't know of a more exciting way to discover—or rediscover—the significance of the Bible for our times. If you stick with it, there is no method of Bible study that is more stimulating, more eye-opening, more rewarding. Even if you wind up in the same place at the end of the journey, with precisely the same beliefs that you started out with, you will not be the same person. As you read and think and talk about these stories, you will learn new things about yourself and the world. This matters. The more each of us knows and understands, the better our chances for living purposeful lives, creating strong families, building solid communities, and forging a more tolerant and vibrant democracy . . . together.

PREFACE
by Rabbi Burton L. Visotzky

The divine power of story should not be ignored. For centuries the storytellers of this country provided verbal fuel for the campfire narratives around which our communities formed. The stories of English literature we all grew up with form a canon for our American discourse. They are replete with references and allusions to the Bible—particularly Genesis—that story of stories of divine power and human failure.

During the two millennia before English literature was written down, the study of Genesis formed the glue that held Jewish (and later, Christian) communities together. Through the process of midrash, the communal study of Holy Writ, the rabbis of old kept the Bible alive and vibrant in their own synagogues, communities, and towns by creative rereading of biblical passages. Group discussion of scripture and its interpretation enabled these students of old to read into the narratives of Genesis the concerns and issues of each generation. From village to village, people studied together, discussed the stories of Genesis, and so doing, illuminated their own lives. Through the shared struggle of study, individuals learned to listen and then to hear one another. They grew to appreciate the contributions and insights of others and so formed communities of readers who valued shared discourse much as they revered the Bible which inspired it.

I have found the study of Genesis no less vibrant and essential as we hurtle toward the next millennium. The apparently simple exercise of studying the stories of Genesis with a committed group of readers has been doubly surprising. The first surprise was that a disparate group of readers—Jews, Christians, Muslims, Hindus, believers and atheists—could be bound tightly into a community by the power of group study. Sharing our insights together and taking the risk of self-revelation that comes with true study linked us to one another as though to family.

The second surprise, which should not have been so surprising, was the spiritual feeling that was engendered by this study. As a rabbi, I feel comfortable identifying this phenomenon as God's presence. Yet I know that there have been those with whom I have studied who would attest to the powerful spiritual experience without committing to God. Call it what one will, group study of Genesis has offered access to two powers that are essential if we are to flourish in the coming millennium: the power of community and the divine power of story.

Rabbi Burton L. Visotzky teaches Midrash at the Jewish Theological Seminary of America and is the author of *The Genesis of Ethics* and *Reading the Book*.

All human beings have an innate need to hear and tell stories and to have a story to live by . . . religion, whatever else it has done, has provided one of the main ways of meeting this abiding need.

—**Harvey Cox**, *The Seduction of the Spirit* (1973)

I am still learning the art of writing from the Book of Genesis . . . Whenever I take the Bible down from my bookcase and I begin to read it, I cannot put it down. I always find new aspects, new facts, new tensions, new information in it. I sometimes imagine that, while I sleep or walk, some hidden scribe invades my house and puts new passages, new names, new events into this wonderful book . . . It is God's greatest gift to humanity.

—**Isaac Bashevis Singer**, "Genesis,"
in *Congregation* (1987)

Be not ashamed to learn truth from any source.

—**Ibn Gabirol**, *Mibhar HaPeninim* (ca. 1050)

OVERVIEW
by Reverend Christopher M. Leighton

During the last twenty years, I have studied the Bible with men and women; believers and nonbelievers; the young, the aged, and those who fall in between; Jews and Christians; laity, clergy, and academics. I have discovered that this book continues to exert an almost irresistible gravitational pull. Nearly everyone I meet, like me, feels the dual forces of attraction and repulsion. Some want to break its grip. Some want to move more fully into its orbit. But to come to terms with the Bible requires flights of imaginative daring that few anticipate.

The single greatest obstacle to the study of the Bible, most particularly the Book of Genesis, arises from our presumed familiarity with the stories. In my experience, nothing deafens us to the provocative insights that echo within the Bible more than the assumption that we already know the stories and have nothing new to learn from them. It is only the people who return to the stories over and over again who hear the contrapuntal melodies of the Bible. These individuals have all at one time or another endured that awkward silence, inspired by the text or perhaps by the One to whom the text points. It is a silence broken only through persistence. A sacred story only seems to sing after the inquirer has stood waiting, disoriented and empty-handed, stripped of everything but those questions, desires, hopes, and fears that are joined to the soul.

For his televised series of conversations on the stories of Genesis, Bill Moyers has assembled a diverse cross section of thinkers, all of whom attend to the clash of conflicting interpretations and delight in the interplay of divergent traditions. They are able to hear the harmonic rhythms beneath the dissonance. This receptivity to disparate readings is indicative of important developments within contemporary biblical scholarship, developments that hold both promise and threat. Here is a living conversation that not only features some new directions in the study of Genesis, but illuminates the intellectual and spiritual ferment of the culture at large.

The modern era has produced the conviction that the Bible will divulge its secrets only if squeezed by professionals. The governing contention of most nineteenth- and twentieth-century biblical scholarship is that every passage is reducible to a single meaning. When subjected to the press of philological, archaeological, historical, and literary scholarship, the story will yield its "real" truth, namely *the* unchanging meaning locked within the original historical context.

While modern historical criticism has produced many indispensable insights (some of them richly evidenced in this project), a growing cadre of scholars is convinced that this approach makes inflated claims, and moves the Bible out of the public square, confining it to the ivory tower. The appropriation of the Bible by the academy has convinced the laity and a good many clergy to abdicate their claims on the text. As Bill Moyers, among many others, suggests, this estrangement from the Bible deprives us of common ground and strips us of a key resource that might enable diverse peoples to speak across differences. A new conversation is demanded, one that demonstrates that the studies conducted within the academic guild by no means exhaust the meaning and power of the Bible. It is time to encourage a diverse readership to struggle with a collection of stories that has in such large measure shaped the landscape of the Western imagination.

Although Moyers's groups include individuals who are learned in the arts of biblical scholarship, the participants offer a range of possible interpretations that undermine parochial positions, including those of historical criticism. These stories will support multiple readings, because in the words of the Talmud scholar Judah Goldin, "text and experience are mutually enlightening." Each of us brings a wealth of experience that enables us to discern truths within the story that others cannot readily see or hear. The interplay of the Moyers groups shows that the truth of the biblical narrative is larger than any single individual, perhaps any single tradition, can imagine. This is one of the most significant aspects of the Moyers series, and it is our hope that readers of this guide will discover for themselves the transformational power of examining Genesis from different vantage points. What begins on camera is intended to initiate an inquiry that will hopefully continue in living rooms, board rooms, community halls, and sanctuaries across the country.

The receptivity to different readings of the Bible promises to enlarge the horizons of our understanding, but an unbridled curiosity also poses vexing problems for people who regard Genesis as sacred scripture. The Bible is inescapably refracted through particular cultural lenses—specific traditions of interpretation, as well as the individual's personal experience—and therefore necessarily produces multiple meanings. How can we resolve the tensions between competing interpretations and determine the authoritative reading, the one that can best help us to define the ethical and spiritual content for our lives? When we are confronted with conflicting alternatives, do we choose an interpretation on the basis of personal opinion, individual conscience, or appeal to tradition? Doesn't this kind of inquiry destabilize the authority of sacred scriptures and undermine the integrity of our religious communities?

These confounding questions have haunted the church, synagogue, and mosque for centuries, but today as never before the reality of religious pluralism makes this challenge not simply a problem of interpretation, but a fundamental problem of religious identity. Distinctive ways of reading and understanding Genesis have evolved within the Jewish, Christian, and Muslim communities. Our indissoluble differences are made plain in terms of the way each of us leans into and lives out of the biblical stories. But the question that remains open is this: Do we Christians, Jews, and Muslims—and those without an attachment to any particular tradition—have anything significant to teach or learn from one another? In reading a common scripture, we share a common border. To what degree are the boundaries sealed? Should they be? Are there ethical and spiritual truths that we can exchange which will enrich each of us? What dangers follow a dramatic increase in interfaith traffic?

Most of us are acutely aware that the battle for the exclusive rights to the Bible has left deep scars. We have only begun to confront the legacy of distrust and contempt that has pitted Jews and Christians against one another for nearly two thousand years. We have yet to fathom the continuation of these complex dynamics in terms of Islam and more recently in the polarization of believers and nonbelievers. To avoid the dreadful excesses of the past, there is a tendency among many Americans to gloss over our differences and to reach for an easy consensus—to pursue a conversation that enables everyone to walk away feeling pretty good about the other—after all, we muse, "they" are not all that different from "us." Yes, we acknowledge, each of us climbs the mountain along a distinct path, but eventually, we will all converge at the top. Yet, do we? In the scramble to achieve a harmonic convergence, many who champion an inclusive theological agenda end up denying the very pluralism they claim to affirm.

The living conversation hosted by Bill Moyers provides us with an alternative model for interfaith dialogue. It tells us that our task, first and foremost, is not to achieve agreement. Indeed, we need to remain highly suspicious of any absolute solutions. To begin, it is more than enough to huddle around a handful of stories and to ponder the ambiguous promises—delivered to our ancestors and now handed down to us. If we can learn to listen to ancient memories and hear how divergent interpretations resonate in different traditions, we may fortify those habits of the mind and heart that will help us to maintain our civility in the midst of intense disagreement.

The stories of Genesis provide a precious, in many ways unique, meeting ground. Taking a fresh look at these foundational stories offers us unexpected opportunities to come face-to-face with both the affirmations and negations that define us—our doubts, our fears, and our hopes. We may find that in a country overwhelmed by its diversity, a dialogue that cuts across religious, ethnic, socioeconomic, and educational divides is not a luxury, but a matter of life and death.

Reverend Christopher M. Leighton is the executive director of the Institute for Christian and Jewish Studies in Baltimore.

A great many people think they are thinking when they are rearranging their prejudices.

—**William James**

The Bible: a book which either reads us or is worthless.

—**Malcome de Chazal**

GUIDELINES FOR A GENESIS DISCUSSION GROUP

Participating in a Genesis discussion group can be a wonderful way to discover—or rediscover—the timeless stories of Genesis. For many of us, these are old and familiar stories—family stories, really, stories about the lives of our ancestors. Others of us barely know them; some of us don't know them at all. No matter what your background, we encourage you to think about participating in a Genesis discussion group in your community. These practical suggestions will help you to begin a meaningful encounter.

HOW TO START A GENESIS GROUP

1 Starting a Genesis group is easy: Just ask some friends and/or colleagues to join you at your home to watch and talk about the *Genesis: A Living Conversation* series. If you don't want to organize your own group, join a group already formed. Check to see whether there is a Genesis group in your community by calling your local library, bookstore, place of worship, community center, or public television station.

2 There is no ideal size for a Genesis group, but many study group veterans say that six to ten people is an optimum number—large enough to ensure a lively interchange and diversity of opinion, but small enough so that each person has the chance to participate fully.

3 The starting point of a Genesis group must be an openness to different points of view. Keep in mind that learning about other traditions (or hearing new ideas about your own tradition) can do more than expand your world view; it can also serve to deepen both your knowledge and your belief in your own faith.

4 A group can be made up of old friends or new; it can include people from many different religious backgrounds or people of the same faith; it can have a leader or it can rotate leadership; it can meet for one or three hours. Although many people feel that Genesis groups are most exciting and valuable when they include people from different backgrounds and religious traditions, others have found sharing the experience with members of their own faith just as rewarding.

5   If you want to coordinate with the series, your group should plan to meet weekly for ten weeks. Some groups will want to watch the show together and then discuss it immediately; others might prefer to meet a few days after the broadcast. You also might consider meeting every other week or even once a month.

6   Some groups may want to continue to meet after the series ends—there are certainly more stories in Genesis to discuss! One Genesis group actually met for more than five years. Then, since they didn't want to disband, they became an Exodus group.

HOW TO LEAD A GENESIS GROUP

You don't need an expert to lead your group. All you need is a group of people committed to (re)examining the stories of Genesis, learning more about their own and other faiths' interpretations of these stories, and exploring their contemporary relevance.

BEFORE THE GROUP MEETS

1   Usually, one group member acts as the initial group leader. Once the group begins to meet regularly, it works well to rotate leadership.

2   When you act as group leader, it's your responsibility to take care of logistical details and to select key issues for group discussion. Choose a few questions from this guide and/or the program that you think will spark lively discussion.

3   If possible, have the ten-part *Genesis: A Living Conversation* TV series on videotape (or watch it on public television); the Doubleday book *Genesis: A Living Conversation;* and one or more translations of the Bible on hand for reference. And if your group plans to do any of the suggested activities, check to make sure you have any materials that might be needed (e.g., recent magazines and newspapers, etc.).

4   Each person who joins the group should read the next section on "How to Be a Good Genesis Group Member." From the beginning, it's important for everyone to understand that the key to a successful and rewarding Genesis group is as simple as following the Golden Rule: Just treat others as you yourself want to be treated.

WHEN THE GROUP MEETS

1 Have the group sit in a circle or around a table. You might begin with brief introductions and then ask one person to read the selected story aloud. Your group might want to listen to several versions. Try, for example, the *King James Version;* the *Revised Standard Version;* and *The Five Books of Moses,* also known as the *Schocken Bible,* translated by Everett Fox. You will be amazed by the differences in language.

2 As you begin to talk, try to keep the group focused on the story itself before going off in other directions.

3 Avoid "expertism." No matter how knowledgeable you are, if you present yourself as "the expert," you will change the tone of the meeting and chill discussion. Remember that this Genesis experience is meant to be different from other Bible study experiences you may have had. The focus here is meant to be on what the members of your group—not the experts—think about Genesis.

4 Lead by example. Listen actively when others speak and urge all group members to do the same. When you speak, try to build on comments made by others. One longtime Genesis group participant recommends asking each speaker to begin by acknowledging the comments of the previous speaker. Whether you agree or disagree with the earlier comment is not the only consideration; what matters is that the prior speaker feel that s/he has been heard by the group.

5 Be sure not to monopolize the conversation—and don't let anyone else dominate, either. Be polite but firm: Don't let people cut others off or "talk over" people who are speaking. Make sure that everyone has a chance to speak. Some of those who've been in Genesis groups recommend choosing an object—a paperweight, a tennis ball—that can be passed from person to person to indicate who "has the floor." While a person is holding the object, s/he has a right to speak without being interrupted. When s/he is done, s/he recognizes the next person by passing along the object. Others say that they've found it helps to use a chess timer: Each speaker is given a set amount of speaking time for the session.

6 Discussion of and reflection about the Bible can sometimes lead to very personal comments or highly charged responses. While it is important to avoid having a session turn into "group therapy," it is just as important to honor people's feelings and personal testimony. Remind group members to respect confidentiality.

7   If questions arise that cannot be answered or disagreements develop, put them aside for further discussion at your next meeting. Ask someone in the group to assume responsibility for doing some research during the week. Alternatively (or additionally), if the Genesis Bulletin Board is in operation, post your questions on-line (at http://www.pbs.org or http://www. wnet.org) and one or more of the people involved in this project will answer within a few days.

HOW TO BE A GOOD GENESIS GROUP MEMBER

You don't have to be an expert to participate in a Genesis group. Remember that the whole point of this series is to encourage everyone—including those with little or no background or expertise in the Bible—to (re)examine the stories of Genesis.

KEEP IN MIND

1   Listen—really listen. If you can really hear what others are saying, the group's discussion will be far more interesting, and you will learn much more.

2   Be honest. People in the group want to hear what you really think, not what you think you should say.

3   Be open to new viewpoints and new ideas. Each of us comes to the Bible with a different perspective. Try to give all interpretations a hearing.

4   Reaching consensus on the meaning of the text is not the goal of a Genesis group. Learning, sharing, and interreligious understanding are. Even when you disagree, respect others—their views, their opinions, and, most important, their beliefs. How you say things may be as important as what you say. Try to say "I don't agree with you" instead of "You're wrong."

5   Don't rush to smooth over differences. Try to understand your differences and honor them. There should be no proselytizing—hidden or overt—in this setting.

6 Don't monopolize the conversation. Remember that you will learn more from hearing others talk than you will from hearing yourself talk.

7 Come prepared. Watch the programs; read the materials; reflect on your own experience. A good discussion depends on every group member bringing his or her best thinking to the discussion—as well as his or her feelings and beliefs.

HOW TO USE THIS GUIDE

Each chapter that follows includes discussion questions, a main essay by a leading scholar or teacher, short pieces on a wide range of related topics, and activities for groups and families. Also featured in each chapter is a two-page spread of a key question followed by commentary, drawn from classical sources as well as contemporary writers and thinkers. These pages create a kind of town meeting across traditions and generations, as do the "Reflections" on the last pages of each chapter.

This guide can give you only a small taste of the work of the remarkable thinkers of every religion and every age who have studied Genesis, and it can suggest only a few of the ways you might engage with these stories. Whether you read the guide from cover to cover or browse through it, remember that this is not a guide that provides answers. Although in many places it suggests how you might find answers, it mostly asks questions and encourages you to ask questions, too.

Enjoy the challenge.

That is what learning is. You suddenly understand something you've understood all your life, but in a new way.

—**Doris Lessing**, *The Four-Gated City* (1969)

GENESIS: THE STORIES

1 IN GOD'S IMAGE

✺ THE STORY OF CREATION: GENESIS 1–2

*In the beginning God created the heaven and the earth . . .
And God said, Let us make man in our image, after our like-
ness . . . So God created man in his own image, in the image
of God created he him; male and female created he them.*
(Genesis 1:1, 26–27, *King James Version*)

*And the Lord God formed man from the dust of the ground,
and breathed into his nostrils the breath of life; and man
became a living soul.* (Genesis 2:7, *King James Version*)

We all remember this first story of the Bible. In just six days,
God—a God of grandeur, majestic force, and presence—made our
world. God brought forth light from darkness, dry land from the
waters, and grasses and fruits and herbs from the earth, and God
created all living creatures, and on the sixth and last day of God's
labors, God made man and woman. Then, on the seventh day,
God rested. Everything seemed complete, and in order. Yet, in
Genesis, there are two accounts of the creation of humankind,
and the relationship between the two stories has puzzled readers
for generations.

——————

Now read both stories in your own Bible (in Genesis 1 and Genesis
2). As you do, consider the following questions:

- What does it mean to us to have been created "in the image of
  God"?

- Why do you think God is called "He" in so many English translations of the Bible? Do you think of God as being male or female?

Why does the question of God's gender often evoke such powerful responses?

- How does human creativity relate to divine creativity? In the arts? In business? In raising a family?

- How have the stories of creation in Genesis shaped our perceptions of women through the centuries?

- If you weren't aware before that there are two distinct stories in Genesis about the creation of man and woman, does this realization change your view of creation? Of God's relationship to humankind?

IN GOD'S IMAGE
by Renita J. Weems

In our Western way of thinking, two stories mean that one is truth and the other isn't. We have a tough time with one coexisting next to the other. It creates a whole host of problems for us because we expect the Bible to be free of these kinds of contradictions.

I remember looking at these two stories on my own for the first time and thinking, "How could I have missed that?" But, you know, when I stop seeing them as actual accounts of what happened I feel better. I am more at ease. Even now, I can't see Genesis 1 and 2 as accounts of exactly what happened at creation. They are attempts at telling us what happened *from* the beginning, not *in* the beginning. They are about the friction between men and women, about the labor and pain in childbirth, about discord in the family. They are about the suffering and hardship and toil that define so much of our lives. These stories, together, tell us of a world created by God that is also full of imperfections.

I think the most interesting question with the two stories of creation is why would someone sit down and include two competing stories in the Bible? It's something that many of us would find inconceivable. Is it an attempt to concede to two different ways of understanding God and creation? This is a nation-building document, maybe it was a way to make peace about competing visions of creation.

It also touches on the inscrutability of God and existence. But that is where language trips us up continuously because a man and a woman are both created in the image of God, and yet God is more than male or female. Our language portrays a masculine God and yet that first story insists that male and female were both created in the image of God and no doubt God is even more than that. Even femaleness and maleness are shadows of the divine being, the divine presence.

But, you know, we spend so much time on the image of God that we lose God's relationship to the image of humankind. It may well be that creation pulls something out of God. Maybe these stories tell us more about ourselves and what it means to be created, to be dependent on God.

Renita J. Weems, a series participant, is a professor of Old Testament studies at Vanderbilt University Divinity School.

QUESTIONS

- Do we—God's final creations, the only ones God formed in God's own image—have a role to play in helping to impose order on chaos? Or is everything in God's hands?

ON CREATION
by Jon D. Levenson

In this essay, Professor Jon D. Levenson suggests that creation, which we often think of as complete, is, in fact, a work still in progress. Moreover, he says, many passages in the Bible imply that creation could actually be reversed. If we refuse to respect the limits that God sets, if we behave wickedly, human beings might actually undo creation and plunge our world into chaos again. And while humans, having been made in God's image, have an obligation to serve God, their special character also tempts them to rebel and replace God s commandments with their own choices.

The Book of Genesis begins with a passage that is austere and majestic in tone and highly schematic and formulaic in structure (Genesis 1:1–2:3). The austerity appears in the absence of sensory descriptions, the lack of detail, that is, about how the things mentioned—including God—look, sound, and feel. Whereas Psalm 104, another account of creation, speaks, for example, of God as wearing a glorious robe of light, spreading out the heavens like a tent cloth, and riding on the winds, the opening passage in Genesis tells of a God Who speaks, makes, and forms, in ways that are literally unimagined—"without image." And not only the Creator but His creation, too, is presented with enormous abstraction, as it is experienced by God, perhaps, and not by the eyes and ears and hands of human beings.

In structure, Genesis 1:1–2:3 is ordered toward the Sabbath, which is its finale (2:1–3). The passage is divided into a set of seven days: six of creative labor and one of repose. The organization of this text around strings of seven and its multiples extends far beyond the sequence of days in the primal week itself. For example, seven times we read that "God saw that [it] was [very] good," but contrary to the first impression of many readers, He does not see this on every day in the seven-day sequence. Missing on the second and seventh days, this clause occurs twice on the adjoining third and sixth days in compensation (1:4, 10, 12, 18, 21, 25, 31). Similarly, the word for "God" occurs thirty-five times, and that for "earth" twenty-one. Thirty-five is also the number of words in the Hebrew original of 2:1–3, the passage about God's observance of the primordial Sabbath, with which this haunting text draws to its fitting close. The Sabbath is, in fact, the apex and culmination of the opening passage of Genesis, and by threading numerous sets of seven and its multiples into the text, the author has powerfully underscored the preciousness of the Sabbath and its divine origin. It is worthy of note that most biblical allusions to creation do not mention a seven-day sequence (e.g., Psalm 104) and most allusions to the Sabbath never mention creation (e.g., Deuteronomy 5:12–15).

In the first three of the other six days of creation, God creates in generalities—light on the first day (1:1–5), the sky to separate the waters below from the waters above on the second (vv. 6–8), and the dry land and seas on the third day (vv. 9–13). Then, in the second set of three days, He creates specific beings that correspond to these more general things and in the same order—

heavenly lights on the fourth day (vv. 14–19), birds to fly in the sky and sea animals to occupy the waters below on the fifth (vv. 20–23), and animals and human beings to populate the dry land on the sixth day of creation (vv. 24–28). Note that on the last day of each set of three, God performs two creative acts and thus twice pronounces the results good (vv. 9–13, 24–31). The last product of His creative labors is human beings—male and female to-gether—whom He appoints as His royal commissioners, charged with a divine mandate to rule over creation (vv. 26–28; cf. Psalms 8:4–9).

It has often been thought that the opening passage of Genesis reports that God created the world out of nothing. Whatever else can be said for this important traditional doctrine, it is difficult to square with the account of creation in Genesis 1:1–2:3. For there we find no report of God's creating water or darkness, which are already present when He begins His creation with words "Let there be light" (1:2–3; cf. Isaiah 45:7). "Heaven" and "earth" are not created before this pronouncement, but afterward, on the sec-ond and third days, respectively (vv. 6–8, 9–10). The notion of primordial waters (Hebrew, *tehom*, "the deep," "the abyss," 1:2) recalls other ancient Near Eastern accounts of creation, especially the Babylonian poem known as *Enuma Elish*, in which the omnip-otent god Marduk does battle with the violent sea goddess Tiamat and creates the world after splitting her body in half. The idea of creation through combat near or with the waters, including the splitting of the sea, is widespread in the Bible, too (e.g., Exodus 14:1–15:21; Isaiah 51:9–11; Psalms 74:12–17; 89:6–15). Against this background, the placidity of creation in Genesis 1:1–2:3 is remarkable, for there God is unopposed, and even the great sea monsters are His own creations, first appearing not when He di-vides the primordial waters (1:6–7), but only on the fifth day (v. 21).

In the opening text of the Book of Genesis, it is not only that God dominates, ordering the world according to His sovereign and unchallenged will; there He is the only one who acts at all. When He says, "Let us make man in our image, after our like-ness," He is probably addressing a council of other deities, but, if so, we never hear their reply (vv. 26–27). He acts in lonely and lordly majesty. What He acts against should not be conceived as "nothing" in the sense of a vacuum but as chaos: radical, godless disorder and moral evil. His acts of creation are equally acts of redemption, and they constitute a stupendous moral triumph.

When He has finished His work of creation, the primordial realities of darkness and water remain, but radically transformed. Now darkness must alternate with light, and water, no longer unbounded, is confined to the seas (cf. Psalms 104:9). Acting like an ancient Israelite priest (cf. Ezekiel 44:23–24), God in Genesis 1:1–2:3 separates things into their proper categories, pronounces on their fitness, and blesses and sanctifies the Sabbath. His finding all that He has made to be "very good" (1:31) does not, however, imply that the radical evil symbolized by darkness and the primordial abyss has disappeared or that reality in its entirety has been rendered inherently good. The world, rather, is neither a part of God nor His enemy. It is something much more ambiguous; it is His creation, and so are human beings, who owe their existence to Him and His mysterious purposes. Their special character, their being made in His image, obligates them to His service, even if it also tempts them to rebel and replace His commandments with their choices.

There is abundant evidence in the Bible that the radical transformation recounted in Genesis 1:1–2:3 was thought to be reversible. By refusing to respect the boundaries that God has decreed, by indulging in wicked behavior, human beings can undo creation and plunge a fragile reality into chaos again (Genesis 6–7; Jeremiah 4:23–28). But neither the ambiguous reality established by God's original acts of creation nor the chaos it replaced is the last word. For, in the end, the primordial sea monster and the cosmic evil he symbolizes shall be vanquished (Isaiah 27:1); the day shall come that never yields to the terror of night (Isaiah 60:19–20; Zechariah 14:6–7); and there shall be a new heaven and a new earth, which so unlike the current heaven and earth, will be a source of everlasting joy (Isaiah 65:17–25). The hopes for the end time are patterned upon the varying reports of the beginning. In the in-between time represented by human history, both God and evil are alive and indescribably potent.

Jon D. Levenson is the Albert A. List Professor of Jewish Studies at Harvard University. His recent books include *Creation and the Persistence of Evil: The Jewish Drama of Divine Omnipotence* and *The Death and Resurrection of the Beloved Son: The Transformation of Child Sacrifice in Judaism and Christianity*.

QUESTIONS

- Do you think creation was wholly completed by the seventh day? Or is creation ongoing? Never-ending?

- If the darkness and the waters existed before God created the world, did the act of creation forever tame these incredibly potent forces—or merely subdue them for a while?

- If creation was about God's imposing order on chaos, what do you think is the balance of chaos and order in our world today? When do you think of your own life as a struggle to make order out of chaos?

A PALACE IN TIME: AN EXCERPT FROM *THE SABBATH* by *Rabbi Abraham Joshua Heschel*

And on the seventh day God finished His work which He had made; and He rested . . . And God blessed the seventh day, and hallowed it . . . (Genesis 2:2–3, The Soncino Edition of the Pentateuch)

In the last essay, Harvard scholar Jon D. Levenson pointed out some of the ways in which the whole first chapter of Genesis builds up to the Sabbath, the day that God blessed in the beginning, and, generations later, at Mount Sinai, commanded the people Israel to remember and keep holy. The following is an excerpt from Rabbi Abraham Joshua Heschel's book *The Sabbath* (1951).

The meaning of the Sabbath is to celebrate time rather than space. Six days a week we live under the tyranny of things of space; on the Sabbath we try to become attuned to holiness in time. It is a day on which we are called upon to share in what is eternal in time, to turn from the results of creation to the mystery of creation; from the world of creation to the creation of the

HOW HAS GENESIS SHAPED OUR PERCEPTIONS OF WOMEN AND MEN?

Man has no part in making woman . . . He is neither participant nor spectator nor consultant at her birth. Like man, woman owes her life solely to God. To claim that the rib means inferiority or subordination is to assign the man qualities over the woman which are not in the narrative itself . . . By contrast, he is formed from dirt . . .

—**Phyllis Trible**, a series participant,
from *God and the Rhetoric of Sexuality* (1978)

Implicitly adopting the male life as the norm, they have tried to fashion women out of a masculine cloth. It all goes back, of course, to Adam and Eve—a story which shows among other things that if you make a woman out of a man, you are bound to get into trouble. In the life cycle, as in the Garden of Eden, woman has been the deviant.

—**Carol Gilligan**, a series participant,
author of *In a Different Voice*

We are then told that, from the very beginning, man has been created "male and female" . . . God [creates woman] in order to help him escape from this situation of solitude: "It is not good that the man should be alone; I will make him a helper fit for him." The creation of woman is thus marked from the outset by the principle of help: a help which is not one-sided but mutual. Woman complements man, just as man complements woman . . .

—**Pope John Paul II**

Woman is more than man's female counterpart; like his rib, she is part of him, part of his structure, and without her he is essentially incomplete. The Talmud says: "He is called man only if he has a wife." However, the Bible does not see man and woman as equals. The Torah is frankly male-oriented.

—**W. Gunther Plaut,** *The Torah:*
A Modern Commentary (1981)

Woman, says the Law, is in all things inferior to man. Let her accordingly be submissive, not for humiliation, but that she may be directed; for authority has been given by God to man.

—**Josephus,** *Against Apion*, ii. 24

Man was not created for the woman, but woman for the man.

—**New Testament: I Corinthians 11:9**

world . . . The seventh day is like a palace in time with a kingdom for all. It is not a date but an atmosphere . . .

The art of keeping the seventh day is the art of painting on the canvas of time the mysterious grandeur of the climax of creation: as He sanctified the seventh day, so shall we. The love of the Sabbath is the love of man for what he and God have in common.

To set apart one day a week for freedom, a day on which we would not use the instruments which have been so easily turned into weapons of destruction, a day for being with ourselves, a day of detachment from the vulgar, of independence of external obligations, a day on which we stop worshipping the idols of technical civilization, a day on which we use no money, a day of armistice in the economic struggle with our fellow men and the forces of nature—is there any institution that holds out a greater hope for man's progress than the Sabbath?

Rabbi Abraham Joshua Heschel (1907–72) was one of modern Judaism's preeminent scholars, teachers, and political activists and the author of many books.

QUESTIONS

- Is there anything in your life that comes close to giving you the sense of "holiness in time" that Rabbi Heschel describes?

- Walter Brueggemann has suggested that the Sabbath is "an antidote to the enormous anxiety we have about the fragility of the world." What, if anything, do you think you might gain by setting the Sabbath apart?

ONE STORY OR TWO STORIES?

Because the Bible is a compilation of stories, believed to have been written at different times, some of the stories repeat or even conflict with one another. The story of the creation of man and woman, for instance, is told twice, first in Genesis 1:27, then in Genesis 2:7, 18, 21–24. Are these parts of one story or two different stories?

In Genesis 1, both male and female share in one divine image. In Genesis 2, male and female share in one created flesh; the human creature fashioned from dust and given divine breath is divided into man and woman. Human community becomes possible as the gift of God. In community, we who are created in the image of the one God can experience the oneness of our common created humanness, our one flesh.

Some have found it confusing to have two accounts of our human createdness, but it is not necessary to choose between them, to privilege one over the other, or to force them to harmonize. Neither witness alone could do justice to the complexity of gifts the Creator has bestowed on human creatures. And, we recognize the truth of ourselves in each testimony. The Hebrew writers wisely understood we need them both.

—**Bruce Birch** is a professor of Old Testament at Wesley Theological Seminary in Washington, D.C.

I'm uneasy about reading across the first story to the second one. Storytelling communities tend to cluster stories. But that does not imply any great intentionality about how these stories fit together. It's much better to elaborate the tension between the stories than to turn them into a sequence wherein the second story overcomes some problems for the first one. In the first account, male and female are created equal; but in the second, there is some hint of Eve's subordination. How do we hold these two stories together? Especially when, with our current awareness of patriarchal ideology, we are drawn to the first story, where male and female are created equal.

—**Walter Brueggemann** is a professor of Old Testament at the Columbia Theological Seminary in Decatur, Georgia (from "In God's Image" program)

I think we read the text wrongly when we read these accounts separately. We have to read the first version and the second version together. The one doesn't contradict the other. The first version gives you the summary: God created, and it was very good. The second story takes you inside the process, and you get more of the tension, the dynamic, the interaction. The second story is not about man and woman in the image of God, it's about man and woman in relation to each other.

—**Roberta Hestenes** is the president of Eastern College in Pennsylvania (from "In God's Image" program)

They are two different stories. In the first story, humanity is created at one fell swoop, which implies man and woman are equal. And it also suggests something about how we read God—that God can't simply be seen as "He." If humanity reflects God, we have to understand that God has both male and female aspects in some miraculous way. But the second story is even more intriguing because not only is woman created from man's rib, man is created out of dirt. God picks up something and makes it stand and blows life into it . . . Both man and woman are much more subordinate to God in the second story. They have a much more complicated relationship with God as well as with each other.

—**Rabbi Burton L. Visotzky** is a professor of Midrash at the Jewish Theological Seminary of America in New York City (from "In God's Image" program)

ACTIVITIES FOR GROUPS AND FAMILIES

1) THE ART OF CREATION

Have someone in your group read aloud the first account of the creation of man and woman (in Genesis 1:27); then ask someone else to read aloud the second account (in Genesis 2:7, 18, 21–24).

Now have everyone look closely at the painting by Marc Chagall *(page 34)*. What does the way that Chagall has positioned Adam and Eve say about their relationship to one another? Where is each of them looking? To whom does the apple in the middle of the painting seem to belong: Eve? Adam? Both of them? Does God have a role in this painting?

Then look closely at the painting by William Blake *(page 35)*. Where are Adam and Eve looking in this painting? What do you think each is feeling? Does Adam seem to be celebrating Eve's creation? Do Adam and Eve seem active or passive to you with regard to pursuing the other as a partner? Are Adam and Eve portrayed as equals? What is God's role in bringing the couple together?

Now compare the two paintings. Which version of the account of creation do you think each of these artists had in mind: The first? The second? Both? Do Adam and Eve seem separate or connected to one another in each painting? Do these paintings teach you anything new about the story of creation?

2) READING THE TEXT: GENESIS AND GENDER

Divide into two groups and assign each group one of the two versions of the story of creation of man and woman (as cited in the activity above). In your small group, *using only your assigned version of the story,* answer the following questions: With just one version, what do you know about men and women? What kind of relationship do you think a man and a woman might have? Who does what? What do they talk about? Do any aspects of your own life correspond to the kind of male-female relationship you've just described? Do any aspects of our culture reflect the kind of male-female relationship you see in your story?

Then have the two smaller groups come together to compare notes. How do you think our world would be different if the Book of Genesis had included only the first version of creation of man and woman? Only the second version? Which version of the story seems closer to your understanding of male-female relations as they are? As you would like them to be? Do you think we need both stories? Why?

3) THE MUSIC OF LOVE

During the week before your meeting, have group members choose one or two of their favorite love songs and ask them to bring them to the meeting. When you meet, first listen to a few of the songs. As you listen, think about these questions with regard to each song: What are the words used to convey the feeling of falling in love? How do the people in the song *know* that they're "made for each other"? Does a third person help to bring the couple together? Is there any spiritual aspect to the relationship?

Now turn back to the two stories of creation of man and woman and ask: How do Adam and Eve meet in each story? Is there a spiritual dimension to either meeting? What do you imagine Adam and Eve's life is like in the Garden of Eden? How does each of them spend their day? Do you think they talk much with one another? In your view, are Adam and Eve

Marc Chagall, *Homage & Apollinaire. (From the Van Abbe Museum, Eindhoven; ca. 1912. Copyright © ARS NY/ADACP, 1991. Reprinted with permission.)*

William Blake, *The Creation of Eve*. (From the Metropolitan Museum of Art, New York City. Reprinted with permission.)

''in love''? Or do you wonder, to borrow Tina Turner's phrase, ''What's love got to do with it''?

➤ REFLECTIONS: ON THE ART OF CREATION

Sometimes I do get to places just when God's ready to have somebody click the shutter.   **—Ansel Adams**

As an artist, often you have to begin with nothing in order to make something. Sometimes I actually have to create chaos before I can even think about creating order.

> **—Hugh O'Donnell**, a series participant and painter
> (from ''In God's Image'' program)

Everything is gestation and then birthing. To let each impression and each embryo of a feeling come to completion, entirely in itself, in the dark, in the unsayable, in the unconscious, beyond the reach of one's own understanding, and with deep humility and patience to wait for the hour when a new clarity is born: this alone is what it means to live as an artist: in understanding as in creating.   **—Rainer Maria Rilke**, *Letters to a Young Poet* (1929)

God is really only another artist.   **—Pablo Picasso**

To create suggests making something out of nothing the way a man makes paintings or poems . . . When God created the Creation he made something where before there had been nothing . . . Using the same old materials of earth, air, fire, and water, every twenty-four hours God creates something new out of them. If you think you're seeing the same show all over again seven times a week, you're crazy. Every morning you wake up to something that in all eternity never was before and never will be again.

> **—Frederick Buechner**, *Wishful Thinking* (1973)

I can do very well without God both in my life and my painting, but I cannot . . . do without something which is greater than I, which is my life, the power to create.   **—Vincent van Gogh**

2 TEMPTATION

⮜ THE STORY OF ADAM AND EVE IN THE GARDEN OF EDEN: GENESIS 2–3

The woman replied to the serpent . . . "It is only about fruit of the tree in the middle of the garden that God said: 'You shall not eat of it or touch it, lest you die.' " And the serpent said to the woman, "You are not going to die, but God knows that as soon as you eat of it your eyes will be opened and you will be like divine beings who know good and bad." . . . [Eve] took of its fruit and ate. She also gave some to her husband, and he ate. Then the eyes of both of them were opened . . . So the LORD God banished [them] from the garden of Eden . . .
(Genesis 3:2–7, 23, *The Jewish Publication Society Torah*)

Adam and Eve and the serpent . . . the forbidden fruit . . . expulsion from the Garden. Even if we don't know every story in Genesis, we can't help but be familiar with this story, in part because of the vivid images that have come to be associated with it—the seductive, talking snake; the Tree of Knowledge with its long, twisting roots; the red, red apple; the flaming sword of the cherubim, barring forever our return to paradise. We don't often stop to think about what the story has meant to us through history or what it means to us today, but this story, more than almost any other, has shaped and reshaped our views about such basic human concerns as sexuality, male-female relationships, moral freedom, and sin. It has also challenged us to think about how we should live—in relationship to God and with one another.

Read the full story of Adam and Eve in the Garden of Eden in your Bible. As you do, consider the following questions:

- What do you think Adam and Eve's *real* sin was? Was it sexual indulgence? Disobedience? Misuse of God's gift of moral freedom? Pride? Denial of responsibility? All of these?

- Are we all condemned to sin as a consequence of Adam and Eve's "original sin"? Or are we the masters of our own fates, free to choose between good and evil?

- What's the relationship between knowledge and sin?

- What are the greatest seductions and temptations of the modern world? How do they relate to the seductions and temptations that Adam and Eve faced?

- How do Adam and Eve's roles in the story differ? In what ways do those differences influence how we understand male-female relations and marriage today?

ON ADAM, EVE, AND THE SERPENT
by Elaine H. Pagels

In the essay that follows, Professor Elaine H. Pagels invites us to consider how different faiths have interpreted the story of temptation in different eras, including our own. She also discusses how our thinking on a wide range of issues and concerns has been affected by this story, from whether we have the freedom to choose between good and evil to what the "correct" relationship should be between men and women.

The story of Adam, Eve, and the serpent, written down about three thousand years ago and probably told for generations before that, derives from one of the most ancient sources in the Hebrew Bible. Unlike the grand cosmological creation account that precedes it in Genesis 1, the temptation story reads like a folktale, with its story of a man formed from earth, a woman made out of his body, a talking snake, a mysterious prohibition violated with disastrous consequences. Yet because it articulates values fundamental to our culture—values that still matter to us—Jews, Christians, and Muslims continue to read it even today, as a story that speaks to the human condition.

Woven into the story are questions that resonate as urgently now as they did thousands of years ago: What is the appropriate relationship between God and humankind? Between men and women? Why do we work so hard—and with such frustration? Why do we suffer? And why do we die?

Many who read Genesis 2 and 3 intuitively recognize that the story bears not only religious implications, but enormous practical ones. The episode that begins with Eve emerging from Adam's body and ends with the man and woman reuniting into "one flesh," for example, has traditionally been taken as instituting marriage. This episode concludes with the comments "For this cause a man shall leave his father and mother, and cleave to his wife, and they shall become one flesh"—words that rabbis in ancient times turned into a code of sexual conduct. Rabbi Eleazar (ca. 90 C.E.) took the first phrase to mean not only that a man must not marry his mother, but also that he must not marry "her who is related to his father and mother" within the degrees prohibited as incest. Rabbi Akiba (ca. 135 C.E.) took the phrase "and cleave to his wife" to mean, in his words, "But not to his neighbor's wife, nor to a male, nor to an animal," thus rejecting adultery, homosexuality, and bestiality. Like Eleazar and Akiba, Jesus of Nazareth (ca. 30 C.E.), when asked about grounds for divorce, answered by invoking both Genesis creation accounts—although his answer, ruling out divorce (Mark 10:2–12) or severely limiting it (Matthew 19:9), clashed with those his contemporaries gave.

Should people today who accept Genesis as scripture follow—or challenge—ancient interpretations? Even in ancient times, among Jews and among Christians, interpretation of Genesis varied enormously. Paul of Tarsus (later known as St. Paul), for example, a convert from Judaism to Christianity, argues at one point that women are naturally subordinate to men because, as he infers from the story of Eve's "birth" from Adam, "man was not made from woman, but woman from man . . . and for man" (I Corinthians 11:8–9). In following generations, Christians fiercely debated what Paul's reading of Genesis meant. Certain followers of Paul actually composed and attributed to Paul "letters" that even exaggerated the patriarchal elements in Paul's letter, with such words as these, written in I Timothy:

Let a woman learn in silence with all submissiveness. I permit no woman to teach or to have authority over man; she is to keep silent. For Adam was formed first, then Eve; and Adam was not deceived, but the woman was deceived and became a transgressor. Yet a woman will be saved through bearing children, if she continues in faith and love and holiness, with modesty (2:11–15).

Many scholars agree that the unknown author of I Timothy was using Paul's name to oppose Christian groups in which women did speak, teach, and wield authority. I Timothy also argues against radical Christians who believed that the sin of Adam and Eve was sexual—that the forbidden "fruit of the Tree of Knowledge" conveyed, above all, carnal knowledge. Such Christians insisted that only those who "undo the sin of Adam and Eve" by practicing celibacy—even within marriage—truly follow the gospel. But those who came to predominate within the majority of churches rejected this claim and agreed with their Jewish contemporaries that marriage and procreation are "cooperation with God in the work of creation." Many Jews and Christians today invoke Genesis 2 and 3 in discussions concerning homosexual relationships.

Others, however, insist that the sin of Adam and Eve was not sexual indulgence, then, but disobedience. Thus read, the temptation story communicates other values besides sexual ones—above all, a vision of humanity endowed with moral freedom and moral responsibility. During the first three centuries of the common era, both Jews and Christians agreed that the central point of the story is that we are responsible for the choices we freely make, good or evil, just as Adam and Eve were. Throughout the ages, Jewish teachers have explained that each person's "knowledge of good and evil"—capacity for moral decision—involves conflict between two impulses contending within us: one good, the other evil. The evil impulse, some suggest, is not so much wicked as aggressive, self-aggrandizing, pleasure-seeking. One rabbi suggests that it may be a necessary element of human character: "Without the evil impulse, who would marry or build a house?" Yet the temptation story warns us to check the evil impulse.

Some Christians, however, later interpreted the story in a far more radical way. The renowned Christian teacher Augustine, writing in the fourth century, went so far as to insist that Adam's sin so infected the human capacity for moral choice that we no longer can choose not to sin. Augustine suggested that Adam's sins irrevocably changed human nature so that our natural human inclinations impel us to sin. This pessimistic view of human nature has been challenged ever since Augustine proposed it. It diverges sharply from Jewish teachings that emphasize human responsibility for good and evil. Yet for countless Christians influenced by Augustine, both Catholic and Protestant, the story of Adam and Eve has become virtually synonymous with "original sin."

Finally the story raises questions about our relationship with the divine. What about the anthropomorphic picture of God as one who shaped Adam from earth and breathed life into his nostrils? To whom is God speaking when he says that "the man and woman have become like one of us" (Genesis 3:22)? Why does the Lord prohibit the fruit of the Tree of Knowledge? How is it that it is not the Lord who accurately foretells the consequences of sin, but the serpent? Was God surprised and disappointed by his human creatures (as Genesis 6:6 suggests)? Did Adam and Eve actually "[hear] the sound of the Lord God walking in the garden in the cool of the day" (Genesis 3:8)? Details that may delight storytellers often trouble theologians. To this day, where some see the picture of a protective and caring divine Father, others have seen a ruler jealous of his prerogatives, who inflicts harsh suffering on his creatures to punish their curiosity. Such questions spurred many readers—Jews, Christians, and Muslims—toward nonliteral and even mystical readings of Genesis.

Even those who do not take the temptation story literally, then, may take it seriously, engaging it to focus discussion as each of us clarifies our relationship—various as these may be—to the issues it raises. Through the process of interpreting, the readers' living experiences come to be woven into ancient texts, so that what might otherwise be "dead letter" again comes to life.

Elaine H. Pagels, a series participant, is the Harrington Spear Paine Professor of Religion at Princeton University and is the author of *Adam, Eve, and the Serpent; The Gnostic Gospels;* and *The Origin of Satan.*

QUESTIONS

- Why does God tempt Adam and Eve in the first place? Was God's punishment too harsh?

WHAT WAS GAINED AND WHAT WAS LOST IN "THE FALL"?

God created man upright; but man, being of his own will corrupted, and justly condemned, begot corrupted and condemned children. For we all were in that one man, since we all were that one man who fell into sin by the woman who was made from him before sin . . . From the bad use of free will, there originated the whole train of evil, which conveys the human race from its depraved origin, as from a corrupt root . . . What is the origin of our evil will but pride? And what is pride but the craving for undue exaltation? And this is undue exaltation, when the soul abandons Him to who it ought to cleave as its end, and becomes a kind of end in itself.

—**Augustine**, *The City of God*, Book XIII, 14;
Book XIV, 13

Free will is bestowed on every human being. If one desires to turn toward the good way and the righteous, he has the power to do so. If one wishes to turn toward the evil way or be wicked, he is at liberty to do so . . . Let not the notion expressed by foolish Gentiles and most senseless folks among Israelites pass through your mind that at the beginning of a person's existence, the Almighty decrees that he is to be either righteous or wicked; this is not so: every human being may become righteous like Moses, our teacher, or wicked like Jeroboam; wise or foolish, merciful or cruel; niggardly or generous; and so with all other qualities. There is no one that coerces him or decrees what he is to do or draws him to either of the two ways; but every person turns to the ways which he desires, spontaneously and of his own volition.

—**Maimonides**, *Mishneh Torah*

We may view all our deeds up to this moment as balanced between good and evil, and hope our answer to God's question to Adam—"Where are you?" (Genesis 3:9)—will tip the balance in our favor among the accountants in charge of the book of life. In this struggle for honesty and courage, for shame and repentance, you should remember that every single biblical hero from Adam to Moses was flawed . . . For each of them shame was not an obstacle but an engine for their greatness. Answering the question of "Where are you?" brought them humility and courage, not humiliation and grace.

—**Rabbi Marc Gellman**, *First Things*, May 1996

In the biblical text, the words "sin" and "fall" do not appear, but "expel" does occur. Expulsion is one phase of giving birth: the fetus is expelled from the mother's body where all that is necessary for life has been provided. It is after the expulsion that life begins—work, exertion, and sexuality.

—**Dorothee Solle**, *Great Women of the Bible in Art and Literature* (1993)

When Eve bit into the apple, she gave us the world as we know the world—beautiful, flawed, dangerous, full of being . . . Even the alienation from God we feel as a direct consequence of her Fall makes us beholden to her: the intense desire for God, never satisfied, arises from our separation from him. In our desire—this desire that makes us perfectly human—is contained our celebration and our rejoicing. The mingling, melding, braiding of good and mischief in every human soul—the fusion of good and bad in intent and in art—is what makes us recognizable (and delicious) to one another; without it—without the genetically transmitted knowledge of good and evil that Eve's act of radical curiosity sowed in our marrow—we should have no need of one another . . . of a one and perfect Other . . . Eve's legacy to us is the imperative to desire. Babies and poems are born in travail of this desire, her great gift to the loveable world.

—**Barbara Grizzuti Harrison**, "A Meditation on Eve," in *Out of the Garden*

ON TEMPTATION
by Robert Coles

At the very beginning of human history, the serpent told us that knowledge was good, knowledge was power, and, even though we quickly learned how high a price we might have to pay for it, knowledge we have desired and knowledge we have pursued ever since. "There is only one good, knowledge," Socrates said more than four hundred years before the birth of Christ. "Knowledge enormous makes a God of me," John Keats concurred more than two thousand years later. But child psychiatrist Robert Coles suggests that knowledge alone is not enough to make us fully human, never mind godlike.

———

The serpent that tempted Adam and Eve, that tempted our forbears after them, still attends us, prompts and prods us, invites us, entrances us: Come, be more than you already are, and do so quite naturally—by affirming and pursuing capabilities already yours. Like Adam and Eve, we are special among the earth's creatures—the one whom the Lord addressed, the one graced with language, with understanding, the visionary one, endowed with ambition and curiosity, whose abilities, ironically, have from the very start been the source of thorough jeopardy.

What the serpent told Eve, promised her, that she and Adam shall be as gods (and with no consequent or subsequent danger of punishment from the Lord), is what we human beings have been telling ourselves ever since—knowledge and more knowledge ought to be our desire, and its acquisition will bring us a kind of divinity: the power, the control, the authority that goes with such understanding. Our history has amounted to a pursuit of that understanding and the result has, indeed, been the unparalleled command over nature made possible by our scientific achievements, with more of them, we are sure, around every generational corner.

Yet our history has also given us no reprieve from our mean and murderous side, no matter all we have learned about atoms and molecules, about chemical reactions, about the unconscious and its workings. A century that has given us a hugely knowing science has also given us nuclear bombs, the technology that enabled mass slaughter in concentration camps, and, yes, the gossip and malice, the slanders and spite that one not rarely finds in university campuses or among psychiatrists and psychoanalysts trained to fathom the mind.

Such ironies won't let go of us. Ezra Pound's enormous erudition, his great talent as a poet, did not give him any immunity from cheap, crude hate. The German philosopher Martin Heidegger's brilliant, learned philosophical discoveries gave him no immunity from a self-serving complicity with the Nazi murderers to whom he truckled. Doctors and engineers and ministers and priests and lawyers and professors signed up with Hitler and Stalin, did their dirty work. Honorable altruists, who have proven to be beyond the temptation of accommodation to brute political power, like our Dietrich Bonhoeffers, our Raoul Wallenbergs, have, alas, been the exception, not the rule. To this day, we celebrate not moral intelligence, but cognitive intelligence and now "maturity" (whatever that is): the very bright, the solid and sound, the "well-adjusted" (to what, though?).

In Genesis 3, we are told that an intellect unheedful of the oughts and naughts set down by the Creator, a prideful intellect that casts aside moral authority, will come to ruin again and again. That story has to this day been our story. When Emerson warned us that "character is higher than intellect," he was addressing Genesis 3—the narrative and moral essence of which is the high cost of egoism, of a striving disobedience that goes ethically unscrutinized. Nothing in today's world suggests that the moral tragedy that Genesis describes, that Emerson found so worrying, is in any way less a presence among us now, for all our achievements. That biblical curse continues to be our daily challenge—how to tame our restless intelligence with humility.

Robert Coles is a child psychiatrist, and the author, most recently, of *The Call of Service: A Witness to Idealism.*

QUESTIONS

- What do you believe is more important than knowledge? Beyond knowledge, what are the qualities that we need to make us fully human? Are there things we might do or qualities we might work to attain that could make us more like God?

ACTIVITIES FOR GROUPS AND FAMILIES

1) THE ART OF SEDUCTION

Either before your meeting or when you get together, have group members look through magazines and newspapers and cut out examples of advertisements, photographs, artwork, cartoons, and articles that use imagery from Genesis 2–3. Be creative: Try to get beyond snakes, apples, and the Tree of Knowledge. What images are most widely used? How and why are they used? In the picture or article, who or what is doing the tempting? How is the seducer or temptation portrayed? As attractive? Evil? Conniving? Fake? Successful? How is the person being seduced portrayed?

2) IMAGINING: LEAVING THE GARDEN

You are in the Garden of Eden, and God has just handed down his punishments to the serpent, Eve, and Adam. Break your group into pairs and have each pair act out the conversation that might have taken place at that moment between Adam and Eve. Talk about who you think received the harshest punishment. Talk about where you think you are heading and what that place and your new lives will be like. Are you excited? Regretful? Scared? Do you continue to blame the other, or yourself, for what happened? Are you angry at God? Do you think God is still angry with you?

3) TEMPTATION TODAY: DEAR ABBY LANDERS

Pretend you write a popular advice column, and write a response to this letter:

Dear Abby Landers,
   I am married to my high school sweetheart, who I've known all my life. We live in a house in the town we grew up in, and my husband Mark and I both work in the community. I am a teacher, and Mark has his own business. I have just won a scholarship to study for a month in Paris. Another teacher here, Dan, also won the scholarship, and he is definitely going. The money would cover Mark's living

expenses, but he says it would jeopardize his business if he leaves for a month. I have always longed to travel, and I'm convinced that his business could survive his being gone for a month. But the fact that Dan is going too has begun to interest me and makes the trip seem all the more exciting. To tell you the truth, over the past few days I have found myself hoping that Mark will decide not to come with me. Should I go, with or without Mark?

—Signed,
Tempted

4) GENESIS AND THE MOVIES: MEN AND WOMEN, THEN AND NOW

Choose one of the movies listed here to watch at your next meeting and/or ask different group members to watch different films during the week and be ready to report on them at the meeting. To look at changing gender roles over time, choose movies that have been made over the past six decades. You might want to consider some or all of the following: *It Happened One Night* or *The Thin Man* (1930s); *Adam's Rib* or *A Letter to Three Wives* (1940s); *Sabrina* or *From Here to Eternity* (1950s); *Petulia* or *West Side Story* (1960s); *Kramer vs. Kramer* or *Scenes From a Marriage* (1970s); *Crossing Delancey* or *Hannah and Her Sisters* (1980s); *While You Were Sleeping* or *Sleepless in Seattle* (1990s).

When your group meets, consider: In what ways do these films reflect and/or distort the gender roles and the ideas about male-female relationships of their time? Do you see any connection between the gender roles and relationships in these movies and the two Adam and Eve creation stories we discussed last time? Do you see any other elements of Adam and Eve's story in the films? For example, is there a paradise—a place, a time, a relationship, a way of life—that is destroyed or lost? Does the hero or heroine struggle with some temptation? What does s/he do about it? Just before you end your discussion, as a group, try to imagine a movie or movies you think will accurately describe male-female relationships during the remainder of this decade.

REFLECTIONS: ON TEMPTATION, SIN, AND REDEMPTION

And lead us not into temptation, but deliver us from evil . . .

—The Lord's Prayer

Lead me not into temptation. I can find the way myself.

—**Rita Mae Brown**

My son, if thou come to serve the Lord, prepare thy soul for temptation.

—**Ecclesiasticus 2:1**

I can resist everything but temptation.

—**Oscar Wilde**, *Lady Windermere's Fan* (1892)

We all have our flaws. Mine is being wicked.

—**James Thurber**

Evils draw men together.

—**Aristotle**, quoting a proverb, in *Rhetoric*

The snake stood up for evil in the Garden.

—**Robert Frost**, *The Ax-Helve* (1923)

As for me, I would rather
Be a worm in a wild apple than a son of man.

—**Robinson Jeffers**, *Original Sin* (1948)

The last temptation is the greatest treason:
To do the right deed for the wrong reason.

—**T. S. Eliot**, *Murder in the Cathedral* (1935)

Perhaps there is only one cardinal sin: impatience. Because of impatience we were driven out of Paradise; because of impatience we cannot return.

—**Franz Kafka**

Men are not punished for their sins, but by them.

—**Elbert Hubbard**

To err is human, to forgive, divine.

—**Alexander Pope**, *An Essay on Criticism* (1711)

To err is human—but it feels divine.

—**Mae West**

3 THE FIRST MURDER

⤳ THE STORY OF CAIN AND ABEL: GENESIS 4

YHWH had regard for Hevel [Abel] and his gift,
for Kayin [Cain] and his gift he had no regard.
Kayin became exceedingly upset and his face fell.
YHWH said to Kayin:
Why are you so upset? Why has your face fallen?
Is it not thus:
If you intend good, bear-it-aloft,
but if you do not intend good,
at the entrance is sin, a crouching-demon,
toward you his lust—
but you can rule over him . . .

But then it was, when they were out in the field
that Kayin rose up against Hevel his brother
and he killed him.

(Genesis 4:4–8, *The Five Books of*
Moses, translated by Everett Fox)

"Other sins only speak; murder shrieks," John Webster wrote in
1623, and Cain's murder of Abel has from the first cried out to
us—and then continued to echo through human history. Although this story cries out, it is filled with silent spaces, enough
in fact that the reader may find herself asking question after
unanswered question.

Read the story of Cain and Abel in your Bible. As you do, consider
the following questions:

- Is Cain alone responsible for Abel's death or must God, Adam and Eve, and even Abel take some of the blame?

- Does Cain's punishment fit his crime?

- What is the legacy of Cain? In what ways do we see that legacy in our world?

- What does this story tell us about violence—in the family, in America, in the world—as we near the twenty-first century?

THE LEGACY OF CAIN
by Reverend Christopher M. Leighton

As Reverend Christopher M. Leighton points out in his essay, leaving so many questions unanswered has allowed for a remarkable number of interpretations of this story over the centuries. Not surprisingly, some interpretations have been illuminative and some extremely perturbing; some have led to greater understanding among people and some to unimaginable horror. But despite so many centuries of reflection by so many people, questions still remain.

Two stories have haunted us and followed us from our beginning. We carry them along with us like invisible tails— the stories of original sin and the story of Cain and Abel . . . I don't understand them at all but I feel them. Liza gets angry with me. She says I should not try to understand them. She says why should we try to explain a verity.

—**John Steinbeck,** *East of Eden* (1952)

In the story of the first murder, we are gripped by what is said— and perhaps more important by what is left unsaid. This is a narrative full of gaps, and readers over the centuries have proven unable to tolerate its empty spaces. In the process of plugging up the holes, a wild assortment of interpretations has been fashioned to serve a variety of purposes, some of them deeply disturbing.

The first story to unfold outside of the Garden presents us with the best and worst of human nature. Cain delivers an offering of some fruits of the soil to God, and Abel follows his brother's lead by sacrificing the firstborn of his flock. This expression of worship was not commanded, but reflected among other things a primal desire to reach beyond oneself in gratitude and wonder.

God responds enthusiastically to Abel's gift but ignores Cain's, thereby creating a puzzle that has occupied generations of commentators: Why does God play favorites? No single answer has ever filled nor will ever fill in the blank enduringly. Claus Westermann of the University of Heidelberg notes that blessing or its absence rests on the inscrutable will of the divine. The story suggests that God is One who both chooses and rejects, and discerning a satisfactory rationale for these decisions lies beyond our comprehension. But his favoritism engenders resentment, because both brothers are animated by the same desire to win God's favor. God's warning to Cain in Genesis 4:6–7 is to face his own motivations and resist the urge to seize what he believes he is still owed. The age-old question that continues to haunt us: Does the murder originate in the favoritism of a divine parent who sets the bloody rivalry in motion? Or, as Professor Jon D. Levenson writes, "does the violence stem from Cain's refusal to accept a world in which distributive justice is not the highest principle and not every inequity is an iniquity?"

The German novelist Thomas Mann offers a different reading. He imagines Cain lashing back at God with these words, "Yes, I have slain my brother, and it is all very sad. But who created me as I am, jealous to that extent that under provocation my whole bearing is changed and I no longer know what I am doing? Art not Thou a jealous God, and hast Thou not created me after Thy image? Who put in me the evil impulse to the deed which I undeniably committed? Thou sayest that Thou alone bearest the whole world and wilt not bear our sins?"

The words of a disingenuous scoundrel? Or the legitimate defense of a man unjustly treated? While the question of culpability looms over the story, the consequences of the murder echo resoundingly through the corridors of human history. Nowhere are the reverberations—and the enduring gravity of the offense—more powerfully expressed than in *The Fathers According to Rabbi Nathan* (Chapter 31): "*The voice of thy brother's blood crieth unto Me* (Genesis 4:10): though he shed the blood of one, it is said *damim* ('bloods') in the plural. Which teaches that the blood of Abel's children and children's children and all his descendants to the end of all generations destined to come forth from him—all of them stood crying out before the Holy One, blessed be He." The story therefore reminds us that "he who sustains one soul is accounted by Scripture as though he had sustained a whole world, and he who destroys one soul is accounted by Scripture as though he had destroyed a whole world."

The terrifying irony of the story resides in the fact that it is in the religious pursuit that the brothers become locked in a violent rivalry that produces winners and losers, perpetrators and victims, but not the harmony and equity that the reader yearns for. The elevation of the younger son leads to the humiliation of the elder, and once established this pattern is played out in the stories of Isaac and Ishmael, Jacob and Esau, Joseph and his brothers, and subsequently with those who follow faithfully in their footsteps—generations of Jews and Christians, Christians and Muslims, Muslims and Jews.

The story of Cain and Abel, like many biblical stories, has invited multiple readings, some problematic. At the conclusion of the fourth century, for example, in Book XII of *Reply to Faustus*, Augustine develops an allegorical reading in which Cain is identified with the Jews and Abel serves as a prefiguration of Christ: "Abel, the younger brother, is killed by the elder brother; Christ, the head of the younger people, is killed by the elder people the Jews." Augustine reasons that just as Cain feigned ignorance when questioned by God, so the Jews practice deceit in their refusal of Christ. Just as Abel's blood cries out for justice, so the Jews stand accused both for the death of Christ and their failure to heed the voice of God in their own sacred scriptures. "The Church admits and avows the Jewish people to be cursed," Augustine wrote. At the same time, he concludes that Cain is not punished with death, and the Jews should also live protected under the mark of Cain, albeit in a degraded condition, as witnesses to the Truth. According to this view, which remained axiomatic for the Church until our own time, the blot of Cain could be removed only by their conversion to Christianity.

Although the mark of Cain was originally bestowed as a sign of God's protective mercy, over the course of time its meaning was inverted and interpreted as a curse. In 1215, under the leadership of Innocent III, the Fourth Lateran Council promulgated legislation requiring Jews (and Saracens) to wear distinctive clothes or badges that would separate them from the Christian populace. The practice signaled restrictions that pushed Jews to the precarious edges of economic, political, and social life. The legal barriers imposed on medieval Jews in Christian Europe are a grim reminder that the Nuremberg Laws in Nazi Germany were not nearly as unprecedented as we usually imagine. The badge of Cain stitched simultaneously onto clothing and into canonical law in 1215, enshrined prejudices that remain with us to this day. But the seeds were sown long before in the teachings of the Church Fathers, most notably Augustine.

Although Jews and Christians subsequently demonized Cain, the biblical account itself treats him much more kindly. God does after all set him apart to protect him. And if he is ejected from one world—the agricultural—he is also credited with the creation of another—the urban. Perhaps to compensate for the loss of one home, he fashions a new foundation of culture. He and his off-spring are said to lay the foundations of our civilization—cities, music, and the technological developments of animal husbandry and metallurgy.

The legacy of Cain is very much with us in both the impulse to destroy and the impulse to create. The story of Cain and Abel prompts us to ponder the tangled relation not only of the brothers, but of the inner ambivalences and ambiguities that define us. We may never be able to explain a verity so elemental, but we do well to ask ourselves what we can make of this double-edged story, and perhaps more important, what can this story make of us?

Reverend Christopher M. Leighton is the executive director of the Institute for Christian and Jewish Studies in Baltimore and he served as coeditor of this volume.

QUESTIONS

- Who plays the role of Cain in the stories we tell each other today? How do we demonize our opponents? Does religion play a part in this process?

- In exile, Genesis tells us, Cain went on to build cities, create music, and make technological advances. What does this story tell us about the relationship between progress, violence, and civilization?

RAISING CAIN: A CASE HISTORY OF THE FIRST FAMILY
by Rabbi Edwin H. Friedman

If you thought that dysfunctional families were a product of life in the twentieth century, read Rabbi Edwin H. Friedman's case history of the first family and think again.

R ecent archaeological discoveries have revealed a "family workup" done by one of the ministering angels about twenty years after Creation. It is translated here from the original.

This is a family of four: mother, father, and two sons, fairly close in age. They came in because the sons have been quarreling a great deal, and both mother and father appear quite helpless to do anything about this. Most of the focus is on the older brother, who broods a lot, is extremely sullen, and is very jealous of his far more successful younger brother.

The younger brother is not aware of his advantage and thus never tries to hide his success, his easygoing manner, or the rewards of his prosperity. The older seems totally unable to understand why fortune does not smile alike on him.

It cannot be said that the parents, both of whom are only children by the way, show any significant favoritism. Yet I am quite sure it is something in their own style of life that is contributing to the very problem they want to solve.

At the beginning of their marriage, both husband and wife seemed to have lived in a very blissful state, naive, it appears, about what was happening all around them. Something, we're not sure what, changed that, and things have never been the same since. The husband growls continuously about his lot and why life has to be so difficult, whereas the wife never fails to remind him of how much pain she went through to bear him sons.

But it is more than their discontent that seems to be seeping down, particularly to their elder son. More pernicious still may be their attitude *toward* their discontent.

Neither husband nor wife seems capable of accepting responsibility for their own destiny. Both are always claiming that their lives would be far different were it not for how the other behaved. The man tends to blame his wife, and the wife tends to blame the environment . . . Neither seems capable of taking responsibility for personal desires, loves, or hates. Each sees the other as causing his or her own pain.

Since neither talks much about their origins (they both seem to be cut off from their past), it is difficult to know how their own childhoods contributed to such irresponsibility, though there is a strong suspicion here that while they were growing up they had everything handed to them on a silver platter. Indeed, each seems to have led a youth totally absent of significant challenge . . .

There seems to be no strength in this family at all, by which I mean the capacity of some member to say, *I am me, this is where I stand. I end here and you begin there*, etc.

It may be this constant expectation that the other should be his keeper that prevents each from taking responsibility for himself. And as long as this attitude persists in the parents, we can hardly expect the boys to act more pleasantly toward each other, still less at times to be watchful over the other. This situation will certainly leave a ''mark'' on one of them.

In a family like this, with no one able to tolerate his own solitariness, or, for that matter, anyone else's, I fear the weakness in the children will never be corrected. Actually, my fantasies are worse. For, if the current inability each parent manifests to deal with his or her own pain continues, I fear that Cain's view of life will never truly focus on himself and, perceiving the source of all his problems in his brother, he may one day up and kill him.

Rabbi Edwin H. Friedman has been teaching and practicing family therapy for over three decades. He is the author of *Generation to Generation: Family Process in Church and Synagogue* and *Friedman's Fables*, from which ''Raising Cain'' has been excerpted.

ON TRANSLATION
by Everett Fox

GENESIS 4:6–7

And the LORD said unto Cain, Why art thou wroth? and why is thy countenance fallen? If thou doest well, shalt thou not

WHAT ARE THE ORIGINS OF HUMAN VIOLENCE?

And he said, What hast thou done? The voice of thy brother's blood crieth unto me from the ground. (Genesis 4:10, *King James Version*)

If only there were evil people somewhere insidiously committing evil deeds, and it were necessary only to separate them from the rest of us and destroy them. But the line dividing good and evil cuts through the heart of every human being.

> —**Aleksandr Solzhenitsyn,**
> *The Gulag Archipelago* (1974)

In its typical and simple form, violence is an eruption of pent-up passion. When a person has been denied over a period of time what he feels are his legitimate rights . . . violence is the predictable end result. Violence is an explosion of the drive to destroy that which is interpreted as the barrier to one's self-esteem, movement, and growth. This desire to destroy may so completely take over the person that any object that gets in the way is destroyed. Hence the person strikes out blindly, often destroying those for whom he cares and even himself in the process.

> —**Rollo May,** *Power and Innocence* (1972)

What does [the story of Cain and Abel] mean for us [in South Africa]? I think the story meant to tell us that oppressors shall have no place on God's earth. Oppressors have no home . . . And so whites remain anxious and fearful. The really frightened ones who are eaten up with anxiety are those who think that peace lies in the insecurity and oppression of the other; those who think that peace lies in the ability to destroy the other; those who think to intimidate the other and to threaten the death of the other constitutes their own security and certainty.

> —**Reverend Allan Boesak,** *Black and Reformed:*
> *Apartheid, Liberation and the Calvinist Tradition* (1984)

To bear up under the pangs of his envy [due to sibling rivalry], the child needs to be encouraged in fantasies of getting even someday; then he will be able to manage at the moment, because of the conviction that the future will set things aright. Most of all, the child wants support for his still very tenuous belief that through growing up, working hard, and maturing he will one day be the victorious one. If his present sufferings will be rewarded in the future, he need not act on his jealousy of the moment, the way Cain did.

> —**Bruno Bettelheim**, *The Uses of Enchantment* (1975)

We are a country that's infatuated with violence. Some of us are in love with violence or addicted to it. We celebrate it. We're entertained by it. We run to read about it, to see it. We encourage children sometimes to fight. We don't want a wimp for a child. In a lot of ways, the cultural issues are as important as the family issues because even when a family is trying to give the right message, a child begins to learn, from outside of that family, different messages. As I travel across the country, one thing I see pretty universally among American children is an admiration for violence.

> —**Deborah Prothrow-Stith, M.D.**,
> Harvard School of Public Health

be accepted? and if thou doest not well, sin lieth at the door.
And unto thee shall be his desire, and thou shalt rule over
him.

(*King James Version*)

The LORD said to Cain, "Why are you angry, and why has
your countenance fallen? If you do well, will you not be ac-
cepted? And if you do not do well, sin is couching at the door;
its desire is for you, but you must master it."

(*Revised Standard Version*)

YHWH said to Kayin:
Why are you so upset? Why has your face fallen?
Is it not thus:
If you intend good, bear-it-aloft,
but if you do not intend good,
at the entrance is sin, a crouching-demon,
toward you his lust—
but you can rule over him.

(*The Five Books of Moses*, translated by Everett Fox)

We are not always aware of how important a translator's choice of words can be to our understanding of the Bible, but looking at the same passage from three different translations makes it impossible for us not to notice the differences. In order to "draw the reader into the world of the Hebrew Bible through the power of its language," Everett Fox has stayed as close to the original Hebrew as possible in his recently completed translation. Here, a comment from Fox's introduction to *The Five Books of Moses*, Volume I of the Schocken Bible, on some of the difficulties of a translator's art:

From the very moment of the Bible's editing and promulgation, there began the historical process of interpretation, a process which has at times led to violent disagreement between individuals and even nations. Everyone who has ever taken the Bible seriously has staked so much on a particular interpretation of the text that altering it has become close to a matter of life and death. Nothing can be done about this situation, unfortunately, and once again the translator must do the best he or she can. Art, by its very nature, gives rise to interpretation—else it is not great art. The complexity and ambiguity of great literature invites interpretation, just as the complexities and ambiguities of its interpreters encourage a wide range of perspectives. The Hebrew Bible, in which very diverse material has been juxtaposed in a far-ranging collection spanning centuries, rightly or wrongly pushes the commentator and reader to make inner connections and draw overarching conclusions . . . (*The Five Books of Moses*, Vol. I of the *Schocken Bible*)

Everett Fox is Glick Professor of Judaic and Biblical Studies at Clark University in Worcester, Massachusetts.

ACTIVITIES FOR GROUPS AND FAMILIES

1) GENESIS AND THE MOVIES: *EAST OF EDEN*

With your group, watch all or part of the 1955 Hollywood film of John Steinbeck's novel *East of Eden* and discuss the following: Steinbeck wrote that he based *East of Eden* directly on the Cain and Abel story. You have been offered the opportunity to do another version of the Cain and Abel story for a 1990s audience. Who would you cast as Cain? As Abel? In *East of Eden*, the director added a female character as a focus for Cain and Abel's rivalry. Why do you think he did this? Would you add such a character to your movie? Consider making the Cain and Abel characters into sisters, rather than brothers. How do you think this would change the story? How do you plan to have the siblings in your movie end up? Will they be reconciled? Overwhelmed with guilt? Acting on dangerous impulses? Indifferent to one another?

2) THE ART AND LANGUAGE OF VIOLENCE

During the week before this discussion, ask group members to clip articles about violent acts from newspapers and magazines. When you get together, pass the articles around and try to determine what motivated the violent acts: Economic stress? Family tensions? Rivalry? Jealousy? How do the news stories relate to the story of Cain and Abel? Does the biblical story shed any light on the violent incidents in the news? Do the incidents shed any light on the story?

3) IMAGINING: CAIN ON TRIAL

Organize your group to conduct a trial of Cain. Assign the roles of prosecution and defense attorneys, judge, and jurors. Also assign the roles of Cain, Adam, and Eve. Finally, assign the role of God's representative or attorney. The remaining members of the group can be on call as character and expert witnesses. Have each side spend a few minutes constructing its case. First, decide what you think Cain is guilty of: As prosecutor, what will you charge him with? As counsel to the defense, will you plead him guilty, not guilty, or guilty with mitigating circumstances? Second, reconstruct the crime. What actually happened at the crime scene? What words did the brothers speak to each other right before the act? What was the murder weapon? Third, consider possible defenses that might be raised. Was the killing premeditated? Was it possible for Cain to appreciate the consequences of his actions? (Remember: There had been no death before this one.) Did Cain know that what he did would be considered a crime? (Remember: There were no laws.) Is Cain the only one responsible for what happened? Who else shares responsibility for the act? (Consider: Adam and Eve, God, Abel himself.) What was Cain's psychological state at the time of the act? Finally, discuss sentencing. What punishment, if any, would fit this crime?

REFLECTIONS: ON BROTHERHOOD AND SISTERHOOD

My humanity is bound up in yours, for we can only be human together.
—Bishop Desmond Tutu

The Bible tells us to love our neighbors and also love our enemies; probably because they are generally the same people.
—Mark Twain

You don't live in a world all alone. Your brothers are here too.
—Albert Schweitzer, on receiving the Nobel Prize for Peace, 1952

For he today that sheds his blood with me
Shall be my brother.   —**William Shakespeare**, *Henry V*

And I know that the spirit of God is the brother of my own,
And that all the men ever born are also my brothers, and the
women my sisters . . .   —**Walt Whitman**, *Song of Myself* (1855)

Only connect!   —**E. M. Forster**, *Howard's End* (1910)

You are our dearly beloved brothers, and in a certain way, it
could be said that you are our elder brothers.
                      —**Pope John Paul II**, visiting the Synagogue of Rome,
                                                    April 13, 1986

When indeed shall we learn that we are all related one to the
other, that we are all members of one body?   —**Helen Keller**

I have a dream that one day on the red hills of Georgia the sons
of former slaves and the sons of former slaveowners will be able
to sit down together at the table of brotherhood.
                      —**Martin Luther King, Jr.**, at the March on
                                          Washington, August 28, 1963

Sisterhood Is Powerful
                      —**Title of a 1970 book**, edited by Robin Morgan

There is no escape—man drags man down, or man lifts man up.
                                          —**Booker T. Washington**

The world is now too dangerous for anything but the truth, too
small for anything but brotherhood.
                                    —**A. Powell Davies**, *Saturday Review*,
                                                    February 7, 1959

Until you have become really, in actual fact, as brother of every
one, brotherhood will not come to pass.
                                          —**Fyodor Dostoyevsky**, *The Brothers
                                          Karamazov* (1880)

4 APOCALYPSE

❧ THE STORY OF NOAH AND THE FLOOD: GENESIS 6–9

Now YHWH saw
that great was humankind's evildoing on earth . . .
Then YHWH was sorry
that he had made humankind on earth,
and it pained his heart.
YHWH said:
I will blot out humankind, whom I have created, from the
face of the soil,
from man to beast, to crawling thing and to the fowl of the
*   heavens,*
for I am sorry that I made them.
But Noah found favor in the eyes of YHWH.

> (Genesis 6:5–8, *The Five Books of Moses*,
> translated by Everett Fox)

In the beginning, God created the world and "saw that it was good," not once, but seven times in the first chapter of Genesis. Just ten generations later, though, when God again looked at the world, God found it so corrupt and filled with violence that God destroyed it by a great Flood. Only Noah, "a righteous, wholehearted man in his generation," and his family were spared.

After the Flood, God vows never to drown the world again. "[In the wake of the Flood, what] has changed is not anything about humankind," theologian Walter Brueggemann has said. "What has changed is God. God resolves that he will stay with, endure, and sustain His world, notwithstanding the sorry state of humankind." But for many of us, God's regret came too late. The notion of God as the unpredictable agent of good *and* bad had already been deeply fixed in human consciousness. So deeply fixed, in fact, that this has continued to be the way many of us have seen God through the millennia—and the way many of us still see God, even today.

———————

Now read the story of Noah and the Flood in your Bible. As you do, consider the following questions:

- Was Noah a righteous man? Do you think he would be considered righteous in our day?

- In what ways is Noah a bystander? A victim? A survivor?

- If the world had become so thoroughly corrupt and full of evil and violence and if God was so pained by it, why did God spare Noah and the animals? Why not just wipe everything out and start over?

- If you had to write the headline about the Flood for tomorrow's newspaper, would it be GOD DESTROYS THE WORLD or GOD GIVES HUMANKIND A SECOND CHANCE?

THE DROWNING OF THE WORLD
by Jack Miles

In this essay about the Flood, Jack Miles struggles with how we come to terms with a God who is both so "gratuitously benevolent" that God creates the world for no clear reason and so "gratuitously malevolent" that God later drowns it for no clear reason. For Miles, reconciling these two opposing sides of God's nature remains one of humankind's greatest challenges.

———————

Why did God drown the world? Traditionally, the rescue of Noah, his family, and a breeding of stock animals has been made the center of the biblical Flood story. This is its happy ending, wonderful material for children's pageants.

But parents who attempt to read the full text of Genesis 6–9 to their children quickly discover that it is not a children's story, not the happy story of a good God rescuing a good man from a natural disaster but of a good God rescuing a good man from a bad God. The horror is that the good God and the bad God are the same God.

Genesis 6–9 includes verses that, as traditionally understood, place the mass drowning in a moral frame. God looks at the world he has made and sees "that the wickedness of man was great in the earth, and that every imagination of the thoughts of his heart was only evil continually. And the Lord was sorry that he had made man on the earth, and it grieved him to his heart. So the Lord said, 'I will blot out man whom I have created from the face of the ground, man and beast and creeping things and birds of the air, for I am sorry that I have made them' " (Genesis 6:6–7, *Revised Standard Version*).

But the punishment does not fit the crime. What have the creeping things and birds done that they should perish because of the "wickedness" of man? And "wickedness" (all translations use an equivalent word) is an unnecessarily moralistic translation of the Hebrew *ra*. The word *ra* is the most general of all Hebrew words for "badness," as general a word as *tob*, the word God uses when he looks on what he has made and finds it "good" (Genesis 1:31). God, as he prepares for the drowning, finds the world bad in the same comprehensive way he once found it good. Just as God was gratuitously benevolent when he created the world, so he is gratuitously malevolent when he drowns it.

At Genesis 6:11–12, traditional translations read like the *Revised Standard Version*: "Now the earth was corrupt in God's sight, and the earth was filled with violence. And God saw the earth, and behold, it was corrupt; for all flesh had corrupted their way upon the earth." The Hebrew word translated, again with a moralizing edge as "corrupt," more usually means "ruined" or "wrecked." An at least equally coherent translation would be "Now the earth was a wreck in God's sight," and it is indeed the earth and not the human race that is so described. Similarly, "all flesh" does not refer to all human beings but to all living beings. What is described is less a moral judgment than an unexplained and frightening change of heart.

Even if we concede that God decides to drown the world as punishment for human violence, for actions like the murder of Abel by Cain in Genesis 4, there is still something profoundly disturbing about his conduct. For even if we grant, despite the absence of any report in the text, that many Cains have been slaying many Abels and that God is righteously aroused at the spectacle, the fact remains that it is only after the Flood that God issues his prohibition against murder: "Shed man's blood, by man be your blood shed" (9:6). It is as if only after witnessing many murders God knew enough to prohibit murder, and even then he had to destroy the innocent with the guilty, infants with adults, animals with humans, in order to make his fresh start.

In the biblical Flood story, an ancient editor has intertwined two Israelite versions of what was originally a Babylonian story. In both versions, the Deity repents and promises not to destroy the world again, but his motives in the two versions are crucially different.

In the first account (8:20–21), in which the Deity is called "the Lord" or "Yahweh," he repents by saying: "Never again will I doom the earth because of man, since the devisings of man's mind are evil from his youth; nor will I ever again destroy every living being, as I have done" (*Revised Standard Version*).

"Evil from youth" means, in effect, evil by nature, evil before being taught evil. The Lord has drowned his human creatures not because of what they have done but because of who they are. He gives no indication that he expects Noah's descendants to be any better than Adam's descendants. On the contrary, he implies that mankind is incorrigible.

What is it that the Lord finds incorrigibly evil about "the devisings of man's mind"? An answer is suggested by the story of the Tower of Babel, a "Lord" story (11:1–9) that immediately follows the Flood story. What the Lord finds evil about the Tower, what prompts him to destroy it, is not that it is immoral but that it is the expression of a creativity, a "devising mind" that makes mankind the rival as well as the image of God. But if the Lord finds his rival so offensive, why, in the Noah story, did he stop short of complete destruction? Why was even Noah saved?

For explanation, we must return to the moment in that story when Noah, back on dry land, makes a burnt offering to the Lord (the first such mentioned in the Bible), and the Lord is pleased by its aroma. The Lord promises not to destroy the world again because, though he knows mankind's devising mind will always displease him, he is pleased by the scent of this one man's burnt offerings. The Lord is like that.

Mankind both pleases and displeases him. By his offering,

Noah does not repent on behalf of mankind. As the Lord enjoys the aroma, he does not require any repentance. We are in the realm of pleasure and displeasure rather than that of morality and immorality.

In the longer, second account of divine repentance, the Deity—referred to now as "God" rather than as "the Lord"—is a moral being who makes a moral covenant with mankind. Having bound mankind in words already quoted (9:6) to shed no human blood, God now solemnly binds himself never again to drown the whole world. The rainbow is to be the sign of this promise. Conventionally, the first pleasure-based repentance story is seen as safely framed by this second more realistic one. In fact, neither story quite contains the other. They undermine each other, and in so doing they leave behind, for all the pages of the Bible that are to follow, a memory of radical unpredictability. The Destroyer has repented of his destruction, yes, but this repentance seems as ambivalent as the destruction itself.

Historically, the Flood story entered the national literature of Israel from Babylon, where it was the story of a good god of dry land and order triumphing over an evil goddess of deluge and chaos. When monotheistic Israel borrowed this story from polytheistic Babylon, it faced a difficult choice. It could cast the flood goddess as a natural disaster which the Lord himself could not stop, admitting an embarrassing limitation upon his power. Or it could cast the Lord in both roles as the bringer equally of weal and woe.

Israel made the second choice; and though the motivation was probably theological rather than literary, the result was a stupendous literary character, one combining immense physical power with absolutely terrifying moral ambivalence. God created the world for no clear reason. After the Flood, we know that he has it in him to destroy the world for no clear reason. God knows this, too. His rainbow is a sign, among other things, that he knows what to beware of in himself. And yet full self-awareness will come only much later when the invincible Creator/Destroyer is humbled by the patience of Job.

Jack Miles, director of the Humanities Center at Claremont Graduate School in California, was awarded a Pulitzer prize for his book *God: A Biography*.

IS NOAH REALLY RIGHTEOUS?

Noah was a righteous man; he was blameless in his generation; Noah walked with God. (Genesis 6:9, *Revised Standard Version*)

The original title of Thomas Keneally's novel *Schindler's List* was *Schindler's Ark*. The image of the Ark was highly appropriate for Oskar Schindler's factory, a safe haven for hundreds of innocent victims of the Nazi Holocaust. A playboy and a philanderer, Schindler was no "righteous man" in the conventional sense of the word: He would most certainly have been condemned to death by the vengeful God of the Flood. Yet ultimately he proved to be more righteous than Noah, risking his own life to rescue people deemed unworthy of life by his own society and peers. Most of Schindler's contemporaries behaved like Noah, blocking out all knowledge of the carnage that was being perpetrated around them, obeying orders in order to save themselves and their immediate family. The best that many could do was to ride out the storm in safety.

> —**Karen Armstrong,** a series participant, from *In The Beginning: An Interpretation of the Book of Genesis*

Look at the difference, says one Talmudic sage . . . Did [Noah] ever argue with God as Abraham did [about the destruction of Sodom and Gomorrah]? Did he ever implore Him to show mercy? Did he ever utter a single word of protest—or prayer? Did he ever try to intercede with God on behalf of the countless human beings who were already doomed but didn't know it? As soon as he learned that he himself was not in danger, he stopped asking questions, he stopped worrying altogether. Before, during, and after the catastrophe, he seems to have been at peace with himself and with God—to the point that God had to scold him and remind him of his obligations to humanity . . . Was he in fact a Just Man? He was a human being who, having gone to the end of night, knew that he was condemned to be free; having reached the limits of despair, he felt himself duty-bound to justify hope.

> —**Elie Wiesel,** *Sages and Dreamers* (1991)

The most striking fact about Noah is that his righteousness is genuine but humane. Unlike many other religious figures then and now, Noah never becomes self-righteous (the great temptation of the righteous). He knows human frailty because he knows his own—he is, after all, the major biblical figure pictured not merely drunken but an embarrassment to his family. Noah is righteous in the true sense: trusting in and faithful to God, even God's strange commands; faithful to his family whom he clearly and deeply loves; faithful at the end to the whole earth, even to the animals crowded on the Ark whom, one hopes, he comes to love. As a Christian, I have always been grateful to Noah. It is, after all, God's covenant with Noah which first opens the covenant itself to us Gentiles. Now that was and is a generous, humane, inclusive, and, one hopes, a righteous act which has changed us all utterly, for Jew and Gentile alike.

—**Father David Tracy**, professor of theology,
University of Chicago Divinity School

These are the generations of Noah. Noah was a righteous man, and perfect in his generation (Genesis 6:9). In his generation, R. Yohanan pointed out, but not in other generations. However, according to Resh Lakish, the verse intimates that even in his generation Noah was a righteous man, all the more so in other generations.

—**Babylonian Talmud**

STILL IN GOD'S IMAGE
by *Avivah Gottlieb Zornberg*

Avivah Gottlieb Zornberg points out in this next piece that it is only after the Flood that God tells a human being—Noah—that he is made "in God's image." Indeed, in the wake of the destruction of the earth, God goes farther, blessing Noah and commanding him to be fruitful and multiply, to dominate creation, and to preserve human life against murder and suicide. But what can these blessings mean to Noah when they come from the God who has just wiped out the earth?

The angels, as depicted in the Midrash, are opposed to God's idea of creating the human in His image; they regard their point as proven after the Flood ("What is man that You should have regard for him?" [Psalms 8:5]). But God is unperturbed. To be in the divine image apparently remains a potential reality, even after the experience of evil and catastrophe. (Babylonian Talmud, Sanhedrin 39b).

After the cataclysm, when human dignity and excellence have been totally overwhelmed, God blesses and commands Noah to be fruitful and multiply, to dominate creation, and to preserve human life against murder and suicide. "Whoever sheds the blood of man, by man shall his blood be shed; for in His image, did God make man" (Genesis 9:6), as God tells Noah.

The power of this passage arises precisely from the tension within Noah's experience. After all is lost, God tells Noah that he is privileged, that he bears the royal seal. Importantly, this is the first time that a human being is specifically told of being "in His image." In the most obvious way, this runs counter to Noah's experience of both corruption and vulnerability: In his time, human beings have demonstrated that they are no higher than the animal.

God's speech acts as a challenge to Noah's imagination. Perhaps human beings contain within themselves a *tselem* ("image"), which is also a *tsel* ("shadow") cast by the greater reality of God? Perhaps, as Ernest Gombrich suggests, painters depict shadows to convey a sense of the substantial reality of the object? Perhaps human beings, too, even in their most unstable moments, act, in this sense, as shadows?

Noah, however, responds initially to God's challenge in a very human way. He flees from consciousness and responsibility, into oblivion. He drinks, gets intoxicated, exposes his body to ridicule and disgrace. The Midrash even notes that he must have prepared vine shoots ahead of the Flood—prepared an anesthetic, as it were, against the pains of survival. But later, when he comes to, he curses and blesses his children for their behavior toward him. For the first time, a human being does as God does: uses language to create and compose a world of negative and positive values.

For Noah, the survivor, at a time when so much around him has been destroyed, the radical question "What is man?" has no answers. For another survivor, author Primo Levi, whose books about his Holocaust experience are classic works, the same question challenges him and allows for no complacent response. Against all reason, in the midst of the tormented humiliation of Auschwitz, Levi finds himself desperately struggling to speak words from Dante's *Inferno* to his puzzled companion. It is as though Levi must give meaning to the question of his humanity in order to remain alive. The borrowed words of Dante, rising up from the brute suffering of the concentration camp, creates a counterworld of rich allusion.

In fact, as the Mishna (the first formulated text of the Oral Law, compiled in the early third century) declares, it is at just such moments of awareness that human life is affirmed as most precious: "Beloved is man, who is created in the divine image. Intensely beloved is man who has become conscious [literally, been told] [s]he is created in the divine image" (Ethics of the Fathers 3:18). After the Flood, after experience of failure and against all the rational objections of the moralistic angels, God insists on reaffirming directly to Noah, the survivor of catastrophe and trauma, his valued status. The content of God's message is secondary to the tone of love in which it is couched—as when a child is reared on constant reminders of resemblance to some admired relative, the exact nature of the resemblance is secondary to the atmosphere of affection and meaningful context.

The additional resonance here of God, as creator, recognizing and reminding the human being of a resemblance—against all empirical evidence—provides human consciousness with a lifetime's work to meet that loving vision with an enquiring and most personal response.

_____

Avivah Gottlieb Zornberg, a series participant, is the author of *Genesis: The Beginning of Desire* and a lecturer in Bible and Midrash at a number of institutions for advanced study in Jerusalem.

QUESTIONS

- What do you think God's hopes for man are after the Flood? What could God hope or expect would be different?

ACTIVITIES FOR GROUPS AND FAMILIES

1) READING THE TEXT: GENESIS AND THE ENVIRONMENT

Read aloud two verses in the creation story (Genesis 1:26 and 1:28) and ask: What does God say humankind's relationship to the rest of creation should be? Do you think that God's giving men and women "dominion over . . . all the earth" means we can develop the earth and use its resources in any way we want? Does God hold us responsible for the rest of creation? Then look at Genesis 9:1–7. After the Flood, have God's views changed in terms of the relationship between humans and the rest of creation?

Considering all of these passages in Genesis, do you think we have violated God's commands or simply carried them out? If we have just been carrying out God's commands, what do you think has given rise to the pressing environmental problems the world faces today, such as acid rain, water and air pollution, global warming, the endangerment and eradication of species?

2) MAKING NOAH'S STORY OURS

In her book *The Noah Paradox,* Carol Ochs recommends this exercise: Imagine that God comes to you, just as he did to Noah, and tells you that, even though God had promised not to, the evil in the earth has once again gotten out of hand, and God intends to destroy the entire world by Flood. Again. This time, however, you and your family are the ones who will be spared. God informs you that you can take as much with you as will fit on a large wooden Ark. In thinking about what to take with you, God says that you must take everything that will be necessary to recreate life after the Flood. You must not, however, take anything that led or might lead to evil on earth, and you should not simply strive to duplicate earth as it is now. Ask yourself: Why do you think your family was chosen? Assuming that you decide to go, what would you take and what would you leave behind?

3) IMAGINING: DISASTER

Imagine that the water supply in your community has been poisoned. Divide your group into two groups of unequal size. Those in the larger of the two groups have settled in a building with enough water to survive for several weeks. Those in the smaller group are outside. They are hot, thirsty, and desperate; they are arguing and pleading to be let in. Have the two groups talk to one another. How will those inside the building decide whether to let the others in? Will it depend on whether they themselves would be endangered if they let more people in? Will they judge the worthiness of those begging to be let in? What happens if you are inside and find out that one of the people outside is your mother? Your spouse? Your child? If the group does not allow them to come in, do you go out? If you survive, in what ways will you be a different person after the disaster? What rationales and mythologies do you think you might develop to account for who lived and who died?

4) GENESIS AND THE MOVIES: SURVIVORS

As you've already seen in the "Commentaries" for this chapter, many commentators argue that, far from being "a righteous man," Noah was, in fact, selfish and callous. Others argue that he was more a victim than a bystander in the drama. But no matter what position they take on Noah before the Flood, the vast majority of commentators agree that Noah emerged from the Ark a changed man—one who was traumatized, plagued by feelings of guilt, loss, and confusion. One explanation that has been offered is that Noah was suffering from the same sort of "survivors' syndrome" experienced by many who have lived through the catastrophic events of our own time—the Holocaust, the Vietnam War, the bombing of Hiroshima.

In order to get a better sense of what "survivorship" entails, together with your group, watch one or more of the following movies: On survivors of the Holocaust, *Enemies, A Love Story* (1989); *The Pawnbroker* (1965); and/or *Sophie's Choice* (1982). On American soldiers who survived the Vietnam War, *Born on the Fourth of July* (1989), and/or *In Country* (1989). On the Vietnamese people who survived the war, *Hearts and Minds* (1974). On the survivors of the bombing of Hiroshima, *Black Rain* (1989) and/or *Hiroshima: Out of the Ashes* (1990).

As you discuss the films, keep in mind what Elie Wiesel, winner of the Nobel Prize for Peace in 1986 and survivor of the concentration camps, has written. When confronted by a choice—anger or gratitude—

> [Noah] chose gratitude. For being spared? Yes. As a survivor . . . he or she knows that every moment means grace, for he or she could have been in another's place, another who is gone. And yet, many survivors are haunted, if not plagued, by unjust guilt feelings at one time or another. At one point Noah must have wondered, "Why me?" Surely he did not think he was chosen because he was a better person . . .

Do you think that the films try in any way to distinguish between those who survived the catastrophic event and those who didn't? The Noah story distinguishes between Noah, who survived the Flood, and everyone else by focusing on Noah's righteousness. Are the survivors portrayed as having a special quality or qualities, whether "righteousness," physical strength, or emotional resiliency? Or is survival, as many have suggested, most often a question of chance, timing, and the kindness of others?

🐾 REFLECTIONS: ON THE ENVIRONMENT

To claim that [Genesis] provides "justification" for the exploitation of the environment, leading to the poisoning of the atmosphere, the pollution of our water, and the spoliation of natural resources is . . . a complete distortion of the truth. On the contrary, the Hebrew Bible and the Jewish interpreters *prohibit* such exploitation. Judaism goes much further and insists that man has an obligation not only to conserve the world of nature but to enhance it because man is the "co-partner of God in the work of creation."

—**Robert Gordis**, *Congress bi-Weekly* 38, April 1971

In wildness is the preservation of the world.

—**Henry David Thoreau**, *Walking* (1862)

Hurt not the earth, neither the sea, nor the trees.

—**The Revelation to John 7:3**

No witchcraft, no enemy action had silenced the rebirth of new life in this stricken world. The people had done it themselves.

—**Rachel Carson**, *Silent Spring* (1962)

To me the outdoors is what you must pass through in order to get from your apartment into a taxicab.

—**Fran Leibowitz**, *Metropolitan Life* (1978)

There are people who eat the earth and eat all the people on it like in the Bible with the locusts. And other people who stand around and watch them eat it.

—**Lillian Hellman**, *The Little Foxes* (1939)

Nature, Mr. Allnut, is what we are put into this world to rise above.

—**James Agee**, *The African Queen* (screenplay, 1951);
spoken by Katharine Hepburn

Praised be You, my Lord, with all your creatures,
especially Sir Brother Sun,
Who is the day and through whom You give us light.
And he is beautiful and radiant with great splendor,
and bears a likeness of You, Most High One . . .

—**St. Francis of Assisi**, *The Canticle of
Brother Sun* (1225)

We abuse land because we regard it as a commodity belonging to us. When we see land as a community to which we belong, we may begin to use it with love and respect.

—**Aldo Leopold**, *A Sand County Almanac* (1949)

Holy Mother Earth, the trees and all nature are witnesses of your thoughts and deeds.

—Saying of the Winnebago tribe

Every live thing is a survivor on a kind of extended emergency bivouac. But at the same time, we are also created. In the Qur'an, Allah asks, ''The heavens and the earth and all in between, thinkest thou I made them *in jest?''* It's a good question. What do we think of the created universe, spanning an unthinkable void with an unthinkable profusion of forms? Or what do we think of nothingness, those sickening reaches of times in either direction? If the giant water bug was not made in jest, was it then made in earnest?

—Annie Dillard, *Pilgrim at Tinker Creek* (1974)

Man masters nature not by force but by understanding.

—Jacob Bronowski

I think it pisses God off if you walk by the color purple in a field somewhere and don't notice it.

—Alice Walker, *The Color Purple* (1982)

When the Holy One created the first man, He took him and led him around all the trees of the Garden of Eden, and said to him: Behold My works, how beautiful and splendid they are. All that I have created, I created for your sake. Take care that you do not become corrupt and thus destroy My world. For once you become corrupt, there is no one after you to repair it.

—Midrash Ecclesiastes Rabbah

We know, then, that the conflict between the human and natural states really exists and that it is to some extent necessary. But we are learning, or relearning, something else, too, that frightens us . . . It is not only possible but altogether probable that by diminishing nature we diminish ourselves, and vice versa.

—Wendell Berry, *Home Economics* (1987)

Assuredly the creation
of the heavens
And the earth

Is greater
Than the creation of humankind;
Yet most people understand not.

—Qur'an

The crisis of global environment has brought people of faith back to Genesis, where moral context and compass are set for the work of rescue and restoration. We somehow know—people of faith or not—that it is more than resources, more even than beauty which we feel moved to preserve here. God made it all and declared it to be good: here is a teaching proportionate to the scale of need and depth of aspiration.

—**Paul Gorman**, executive director of the National
Religious Partnership for the Environment

5 CALL AND PROMISE

✍ THE STORY OF ABRAHAM AND SARAH:* GENESIS 11–13

The Lord said to Abraham, "Go forth from your native land and from your father's house to the land that I will show you." (Genesis 12:1, *The Jewish Publication Society Torah*)

Try to imagine it: You and your wife are a long-married couple in your seventies, childless, living in the land of Haran, when you hear a voice that you believe is God's voice. God is telling you to pack up and leave your home and your country for a new (unnamed) land, which God will show you. If you do this, God says, you and your (unborn) offspring will be blessed. "I will make of you a great nation . . . I will make your name great, and you shall be a blessing." What do you do? If you are Abraham, convinced that God is calling you, then you, your wife Sarah, and your nephew Lot, get your household goods together, and you follow where God leads.

———

Now read the story of God's call to Abraham and the first part of Abraham and Sarah's journey in your Bible. As you do, consider the following questions:

- What does it mean to be chosen? Were Abraham *and* Sarah chosen? Is chosenness accompanied by some moral obligation?

- If someone is chosen, does it necessarily mean that others are "unchosen"?

*Later, in Genesis 17, God changes Abram and Sarai's names to Abraham ("father of many nations") and Sarah ("princess") in recognition of the covenant God makes with them. Despite the importance of these and other name changes in Genesis, however, we use the most familiar names throughout this guide—Abraham, Sarah, Jacob—in order to avoid confusion.

- We may see ourselves as following in Abraham's footsteps and continuing his journey, but do we, his twentieth-century descendants, still hear the voice of God?

- In contemporary times, how can we tell the difference between a prophet and a madman, between a call that's authentic and one that's imagined?

❧⸲ HEARING GOD'S CALL
by Sandee Brawarsky

Abraham did answer God's call, and the rest is history—our history. Because when the man who was to become the father of three of the world's great religions set out from his home in response to God's call, it was just the first step down a long road, a road that millions of Abraham's descendants—Jews, Christians, and Muslims—are still traveling today as a result of his faith and obedience. In this essay, writer Sandee Brawarsky explores the nature of Abraham's call and the nature of his spiritual journey.

〜⸲ϟ⸲〜

I t's easy to imagine a Cecil B. De Mille–style call: God's booming voice echoes over the mountains, bracketed by thunder, mysteriously heard only by Abraham. But perhaps the pronouncement is whispered, and Abraham isn't sure whether it is God's words or the murmurs of his soul. Daring in his faith, he chooses to believe that the message is ultimately from God, and he complies. "His faith in following the voice marks the first step on the path we still seek to walk," Rabbi Arthur Green has written.

According to instructions, Abraham goes out from his land and his father's house, not certain where he is headed, but ready to be led by a God known only to him. At some point he stops leaving and begins the long process of arriving, which will engage him for the rest of his days. Although he is seventy-five years old, it is this point in his life that modern observers might define as his coming-of-age; his sense of self is transformed. In fact, when he is called by God, he is living in the city of Haran, which can be translated as "route," "journey," or "crossroads." Indeed, the moment is the crossroads of Abraham's life, as he begins a journey like no other.

Commentators on the text have read God's brief charge to Abraham, "*Lech lecha,*" in various ways, with different emphases and meanings—as "Go," "Go forth," "Get thee out," "Go for yourself (for your own benefit)," "Go by yourself," "Go your own way," "Go-you-forth." The Zohar, the thirteenth-century Jewish mystical text, interprets the text as "Go to your self, know your self, fulfill your self." Abraham must understand his own soul in order to move ahead; it's a sacred journey inward as well as to the promised land. As biblical scholar E. A. Speiser has written: "It was the start of an epic voyage in search of spiritual truth, a quest that was to constitute the central theme of all biblical history."

Does Abraham look back? Do his courage and faith endure? Does he miss the security of his old life and long for its simplicity? It's never easy to break entirely with one's past, with one's family. However, losses are inextricably connected to growth. For Abraham, leaving home is a valuable and fruitful loss. God provides the road map, in a code he must learn to decipher.

Abraham's actions might seem to resemble those of the thousands who flocked to America's still unsettled Western lands, hearkening to the call "Go West!," and the countless peoples who have uprooted their families in search of a better life in a new and unknown place. But it is not the pursuit of wealth or power or adventure that seems to motivate Abraham, rather his faith in God. His reward is the promise of the future, the divine blessing granted through him to his descendants. However, God's words are cloaked in mystery, for he and Sarah are old and childless when they leave Haran.

Why does God select an older man as the conduit of his blessing? Perhaps God sees a blend of enlightenment and openness in Abraham, who has reached elderhood, which Rabbi Zalman Schacter-Shalomi characterizes as "the time for harvesting the wisdom of a lifetime." Perhaps it is Abraham's life experience and his accumulated memory that enable him not only to hear God's call but to act on it.

Do we, the many descendants of Abraham, continue to hear God's voice? Are there certain times of life when God's voice is clearest? Do we need to be in solitude—or is it possible to be called by God while on a crowded city street? Are there calls that we sometimes just don't hear? Or don't want to hear? In contemporary times, some speak of their "calling" as a message of vocation; they view their choice of life's work as God-inspired. Some people encounter God's words in their personal lives, in the kinds of transcendent moments Vaclav Havel, playwright and former president of the Czech Republic who had been jailed as a dissident, describes in a letter to his wife from prison as " 'islands of meaning' in the ocean of our struggling, the meaning of lanterns whose light is cast into the darkness of our life's journey, illuminating all the many meanings of its direction." According to the Midrash, it was God, "Life of all worlds," who "illumined Abraham's path wherever he went."

In our own lives, those moments of clarity—when, perhaps, divinity is our light and compass—are the most significant signposts on our journeys. To novelist and theologian Frederick Buechner, "life itself can be thought of as an alphabet by which God graciously makes known his presence and purpose and power among us. Like the Hebrew alphabet, the alphabet of grace has no vowels, and in that sense his words to us are always veiled, subtle, cryptic, so that it is left to us to delve their meaning, to fill in the vowels, for ourselves by means of all the faith and imagination we can muster. God speaks to us in such a way, presumably, not because he chooses to be obscure but because, unlike a dictionary word whose meaning is fixed, the meaning of an incarnate word is the meaning it has for the one it is spoken to, the meaning that becomes clear and effective in our lives only when we ferret it out for ourselves." (from *The Sacred Journey*)

Abraham could not have known God so deeply had he stayed home. The call comes to us—that is the blessing of God's grace. We rise to answer the call—that is the blessing of human engagement.

Sandee Brawarsky, a journalist and editor, is the book critic of *The Jewish Week*, and served as coeditor of this volume.

QUESTIONS

- Why do you think God chose an older man to be the recipient of this blessing? What qualities and life experiences might the older

Abraham have had that the younger Abraham could not have had yet?

- What kind of spiritual journey is Abraham engaged in? Was Sarah also engaged in a spiritual journey? Do you think their faith was strengthened as a result of their journeying? What is the nature of your spiritual journey?

HEEDING GOD'S CALL: A PERSONAL TESTIMONY
by Reverend Eugene Rivers III

For Reverend Eugene Rivers III, God's call is as real as the inner-city streets where he lives and works.

Т he notion of a call shapes my entire life.

I know that many people feel called by God. If you go, say, to one of the Pentecostal churches in Harlem on a Friday night, you'll hear many people say, "I heard the voice of God. I spoke to the Divine, and the Divine spoke to me." For a substantial number of people, that's a very vivid reality.

If you believe in the call or you believe that the promise has been made, then you see the situation through the eyes of faith. That's what the life of faith is about. I identify with Abraham's call. I also identify with his frailty and humanity. And I identify with the same type of nationalism he did, if you define nationalism as the recognition of a call to be a people, which is related to history, tradition, place.

In the context of my community—the American black community—I see a community completely coming apart in every way. Disarray, confusion, nihilism, and decay—that's what I see. Using Abraham's experience as a model, I could say of the black community that there is no land, there are no people. But there is history, and there are traditions. And there is a call and a promise. So I have a decision to make: Will I obey as a person of faith? Because it's only on that basis that a people will come into existence.

I feel God's demands on me, and I have a very intense sense of God's immediate presence in my life. Because of my work in poor neighborhoods, my home has been shot into twice over the last six years. When this last happened, a church van that was parked in front of our building was shot twenty times. One of the bullets landed within twelve inches of my son's head. My wife and I asked ourselves whether we should leave the neighborhood. The issue of "the call" came up—and it was our personal relationship with a personal God that determined the choice that we made. I asked my wife to decide and she said: "I believe that God has called us to this place to do this thing for this season." We stayed. We felt and feel called.

The notion of a call brings with it a sense of chosenness and also, as the biblical literature suggests must be the case, an equally intense notion of responsibility and accountability. I love the fact that from this story of Abraham I know that an eternal God may be in conversation with the most broken, mischievous, pragmatic, and self-centered individual among us—and that, on other occasions, the same individual, inspired by God, can be elevated to heights of heroism.

Reverend Eugene Rivers III, a series participant, is pastor of the Azusa Christian Community in Boston and a founding member of the Ten-Point Coalition. He has been a fellow at the Center for the Study of Values in Public Life at Harvard Divinity School.

QUESTIONS

- What does it mean to be "called" by God today? Have you ever felt "called" to anything? If so, what did you feel called to? Was it God who called you? How have you responded to the call?

RECOGNIZING GOD'S CALL
by Martin E. Marty

Perhaps the patriarchs didn't ask themselves this question, but more than likely even they did: How on earth can we tell if a call is real? In this short essay, Professor Martin E. Marty ponders the characteristics of a genuine call.

⸻⸱⋇⸱⸻

The beginning of the story of Abraham is brisk: "Now the Lord said to Abraham, 'Go' . . . So Abraham went." Go: That meant leaving land, clan, relatives, and immediate family. He went: That meant heading a great nation and becoming a blessing to all the families of the earth.

The story of Abraham is "only a story," say some scholars. But to most of the three billion people who are "Abrahamic"—Jews, Christians, and Muslims—that story shapes much of their lives and gives meaning to their hopes. Often these children of Abraham are not a blessing to each other: The accounts of crusades and jihads and holy wars involve them fighting with each other as much as with others. But you cannot talk them out of the notion that the call to Abraham made them a people with special blessings and responsibilities. If we agree on nothing else, we can agree that the call was fateful.

Most of the time, we slide too fast over the little words "the Lord said . . ." Should we trust a story that finds God saying something and half of the human race changing because a man heard what God said? There is no claim here that there were stone tablets or scrolls or other physical evidences of God saying anything in writing. "God said." That means: Abraham heard voices—or a voice. Should we trust the story, the voice? Does it come to others? To us? Keep your guard up and your fingers crossed. Who hears voices now? First, the fanatic. The fanatic has been defined as someone who knows he's doing what the Lord would do if the Lord were also in possession of the facts. Second, people with schizophrenia hear voices, sometimes a voice of the Lord. Third, religious prophets and apostles—in scriptures past and in contemporary life—hear them.

Most believers give a special status to the calls of long ago, attested to in the various scriptures. Today, though, self-proclaimed "prophets"—a David Koresh or a Jim Jones—claim to hear such a call and death follows. Founders of many new religions, most of them ephemeral, claim to hear such a call and delusion or frustration follows. You cannot talk them out of their claims, but

WHO ARE THE CHILDREN OF ABRAHAM?

For it is through Isaac that your name will be carried on.
(Genesis 21:12, *The Jerusalem Bible*)

Abraham is unique in the history of religion in being regarded as the "father" of the three great monotheistic traditions of the West. Jews, Christians, and Muslims have all proclaimed loudly over time that their people have the honor of being Abraham's most authentic descendants. Each tradition sees in Abraham the highest expression of the virtues it prizes most highly, but these qualities are by no means identical.

Judaism sees in abraham an iconoclast who had the courage to literally break the idols of the polytheistic culture he was born into and to recognize and respond to the call of the One God, Ruler of the Universe, when it came. This recognition by Abraham was sealed and consolidated through a covenant with God, a covenant that promised Abraham, the first patriarch, and his descendants both the land of Canaan and the founding of a "great nation."

Christianity, for its part, sees Abraham as the father of a religious faith whose ancestry and community are not determined by genetic or cultural-ethnic ties but purely by spiritual allegiance. Its vision of Abraham strongly suggests that the patriarch's faith in God's promise anticipates the hopes of humankind fulfilled in Jesus Christ's life, especially in his death and resurrection.

For Islam, Abraham is the model of perfect obedience to the One God, Allah. In Islam, the claim of being related to Abraham is derived from one's aptitude for submission (in Arabic, the word for "submission" is "Islam"), the submersion of the self in the path sealed by the Prophet Muhammad.

Thus Abraham "believed God, and it was credited to him as righteousness." Realize then that it is those who have faith who are children of Abraham. Scripture, which saw in advance that God would justify the Gentiles by faith, foretold the good news to Abraham, saying, "Through you shall all the nations be blessed."

—**New Testament: Galatians 3:6–8**

People of the Book! Why do you dispute concerning Abraham? The Torah was not sent down, neither the Gospel, but after him. What, have you no reason? . . . No, Abraham in truth was not a Jew, neither a Christian; but he was a Muslim and one pure of faith; certainly he was never of the idolaters. Surely those people standing closest to Abraham are those who followed him, and his Prophet [Muhammad], and those who believe; and God is the Protector of the believers.

—**Qur'an, Surah III:65–67**

God promised Abraham, and those that were righteous of his progeny, to become religious leaders (*imams*) to the rest of the world (Qur'an 2:124). Thus, having a progeny became part of the Abrahamic task of spreading the Truth. This is why Abraham and Ishmael built together the first House of God on earth, the Ka'ba.

—**Azizah al-Hibri**, a series participant, is a professor of law at the University of Richmond

But we are Your people, partners to Your covenant, descendants of Your beloved Abraham to whom You made a pledge on Mount Moriah. We are the heirs of Isaac, his son bound upon the altar. We are Your firstborn people, the congregation of Isaac's son Jacob whom You named Israel and Jeshurun, because of Your love for him and Your delight in him.

—**Morning services**, *Siddur Sim Shalom* (Jewish prayer book), edited and translated by Rabbi Jules Harlow (1985)

In a world which is divided, incessantly threatened and all too often shaken by rivalry and hostility among nations, it therefore seems more than ever time for those who see "Abraham the believer" as the founder of their own religion, indeed of their very selves, to come together as brothers and sisters in a peaceful way. Why should Jews, Christians, and Muslims then not work together to create a world of brothers and sisters?

—**Manifesto of the Fraternité d'Abraham**, the Brotherhood of Abraham, a group involved in the work of interreligious understanding in France since 1967 only a few or a few thousand follow, so taking their claims seriously is not an issue for virtually all of the human race.

So it comes to ordinary people. Do they—do "we"—hear "the Lord said . . ."? Should they—should "we"—follow? Not being Abraham, how should we think of a "call"? How do we test one, if it comes? Most of the scriptures that talk about God talking also teach skepticism along with faith: "Test the spirits, to see whether they are of God." So the best advice is: If the call is too direct, too "miraculous"-sounding, beware. Through the centuries, the people who most felt called and did most with their call found their vocation not through a voice from the clouds or the mountains or even within themselves. Instead, they saw their whole lives as grounded in the mysterious care of a loving God, who does leave traces in history: in events, in scriptures, in the calls and demands of other people, in the faithful heart.

The serious people, at the end of whose life one can observe that they sensed a divine call, tend to be those who let God speak through a million little particulars in life. Odds are, those who lived their lives in response to such a demand and promise were challenged along the way by others. How can you tell if you or someone else was divinely called? Never rule out the possibility that a sense of a call and a calling will be a positive good: The world gets changed, often for the better, because of such responses. Trust the half-certain more than the cocksure; those who test their call in community more than those who go it alone. And never completely uncross your fingers or let your guard down: Response to the call can be dangerous, as many victims of called and chosen people and peoples could have attested. So, the story of Abraham and Sarah challenges, disturbs, and inspires us; it can change our ordinary lives and make us extraordinarily, if cautiously, responsive.

Martin E. Marty is the Fairfax M. Cone Distinguished Service professor at the University of Chicago and author of many books on religious and cultural themes.

QUESTIONS

- Martin E. Marty says that some people who have responded to calls from God have changed the world for the better. When you think about this, who comes to mind?

✎ ACTIVITIES FOR GROUPS AND FAMILIES

1) THE ART OF LEAVING (PART 1)

During the week before you meet, look for news reports, photographs, songs, films, books, or examples from history about families or groups that pulled up stakes and moved from a familiar place to a new, unknown home. (Think about your own parents or grandparents, Americans settling the West, the great migration of African Americans from the rural South to Northern cities, and immigrants coming to the United States.) Why did these people move? Did they believe they were fulfilling a personal destiny? A collective destiny? Have you ever picked up and moved to a new place? How do these historical and fictional accounts compare with your own or your family's experiences?

2) IMAGINING: SARAH'S STORY

There are only a few times when the Book of Genesis records what Sarah said or thought. As a group, read aloud the episode involving Sarah, Abraham, and Pharaoh in Genesis 12:11–20, and then ask two group members to act out the conversation that might have taken place between Sarah and Pharaoh. Where are they? What are they doing? Are they alone? How does Pharaoh find out that Sarah is Abraham's wife, not his sister? Why was Pharaoh willing to send Abraham and Sarah away without punishment, indeed, enriched with gifts?

Now have two different group members act out the conversation that might have taken place between Sarah and Abraham as Pharaoh's men escorted them away from Egypt. How might each make sense of what has just happened to them? To what does each attribute their survival? How might Sarah feel about Abraham's putting her at risk in order to save himself? In order to profit from the transaction with Pharaoh?

How do you think Sarah feels about all of her and Abraham's wanderings up to this point? Does she want to go on? Does she feel included in God's blessing? Is she still hopeful or has she despaired of ever having a child to carry on the promised blessing? Does the story change for you when you can hear Sarah's voice? In what ways?

3) SAYING GOOD-BYE

Tape a big piece of paper up on the wall, then turn to Genesis 12:1 and have someone read the verse aloud to the group. (If possible, read the same verse from several other versions of the Bible, too.) Ask people to identify all the things that Abraham is leaving behind according to the passage and list them on the left-hand side of the paper. On the right-hand side of the paper, list all the promises that God then makes to Abraham. Then hand out blank paper to everyone and have group members spend a few minutes writing down their thoughts about why Abraham decided to go. What is driving him? What might hold him back? What do you think he hopes to find and achieve? Is Abraham interested in acquiring wealth and possessions? Enjoying an adventure? Finding a way to finally have children? Serving God? What is his understanding of the content of God's blessing? Are there responsibilities that go along with that blessing? Do you think Abraham knew God before this meeting? Do you think Abraham trusts God? Do you think he trusts himself? Does he know why God has chosen him? Using people's notes, as a group write a farewell letter from Abraham to the family and friends he is leaving behind.

REFLECTIONS: ON LEAVING HOME

Everyone's always talking about people breaking into houses . . . but there are more people in the world who want to break out of houses.
                              —Thornton Wilder, *The Matchmaker* (1954)

To leave is to die a little.   **—French proverb**

For it was only when they were on the move that Americans could feel anchored in their memories.
                              —Norman Mailer, *The Armies of the Night* (1968)

When you come to a fork in the road, take it.
                              —Yogi Berra (attributed)

Should we have stayed at home, wherever that may be?
                              —Elizabeth Bishop, *Questions of Travel* (1965)

One may know the world without going out of doors
One may see the Way of Heaven without looking through the
   windows
The further one goes, the less one knows.

                                                —Lao-tzu

Two roads diverged in a wood, and I—
I took the one less traveled by,
And that has made all the difference.

                        —Robert Frost, *The Road Not Taken* (1916)

The longest journey
Is the journey inwards
Of him who has chosen his destiny.

                        —Dag Hammarskjöld, *Markings* (1964)

There comes a time in a man's life when to get where he has to
go—if there are no doors or windows—he walks through a wall.

                        —Bernard Malamud, *Rembrandt's Hat* (1972)

To travel hopefully is a better thing than to arrive.

                        —Robert Louis Stevenson, *El Dorado* (1881)

You Can't Go Home Again.
                                —Thomas Wolfe, title of book (1940)

We shall not cease from exploration
And the end of all our exploring
Will be to arrive where we started
And to know the place for the first time.

                        —T. S. Eliot, *Little Gidding* (1942)

Stay home and be decent.

                                        —Wendell Berry

Escape the birthplace; walk into the world . . .

                        —Muriel Rukeyser, *Secrets of*
                        American Civilization (1973)

It is good to have an end to journey towards; but in the end, it is the journey itself that makes the difference.

—Ursula K. Le Guin

Make voyages!—Attempt them!—there's nothing else . . .

—Tennessee Williams, *Camino Real* (1953)

6 A FAMILY AFFAIR

🖋 THE STORY OF ABRAHAM, SARAH, AND HAGAR: GENESIS 16–17, 21

Now Sarah, Abraham's wife, had borne him no children. But she had an Egyptian maidservant named Hagar; so she said to Abraham, "The Lord has kept me from having children. Go, sleep with my maidservant; perhaps I can build a family through her." [Abraham] slept with Hagar and she conceived. (Genesis 16:1–4, *New International Version*)

By the time this story begins, Abraham and Sarah had been waiting for many years and God still had not given them a son to inherit the blessing. Sarah, already well past the age of childbearing herself, decides she might still be "built-up with sons" through her handmaiden, an Egyptian slave named Hagar. But Sarah comes to regret her decision almost immediately. Even before Ishmael's birth, she senses that Hagar's son may be Abraham's, but he will not be hers. Eventually, the story draws to a not-unhappy close—Sarah has miraculously given birth to Isaac, the long-promised heir to the blessing; Hagar and Ishmael have been freed from slavery and are living with God's protection and His assurance that Ishmael too will become "a great nation." But what happens before then, especially what takes place among Sarah, Hagar, and Abraham, is more troubling.

———————

Now read the story of Abraham, Sarah, and Hagar in your Bible. As you do, consider the following questions:

- Why doesn't the experience of being oppressed make it impossible for us to oppress others?

- Does the story tell us anything about how the children of Hagar and the children of Sarah might work out their futures—together and peacefully—as the twentieth century draws to a close?

SARAH AND HAGAR
by Tikva Frymer-Kensky

In her essay, Professor Tikva Frymer-Kensky focuses primarily on the relationship between Sarah and Hagar. Their story, Frymer-Kensky says, reminds us that a history of oppression is no guarantee that we will not become oppressors ourselves and that the destiny of one nation is always intimately bound up with the destiny of others.

The Sarah and Hagar story stands at the center of the Abraham–Sarah cycle, between the two covenants of Genesis 15 and 17 and midway between the *"Lech lecha"* (*"Go!"*) of the call to Abraham (Genesis 12) and the *"Lech lecha"* (*"Go!"*) of the call to Abraham to sacrifice Isaac (Genesis 22).

The story revolves around the relationship of two women dependent on the will of one man, the head of the household. Powerlessness does not unite the powerless: It pits them against each other. Sarah and Hagar are rivals, and Sarah has all the advantages. She is the full, free wife; Hagar is a slave. When Sarah does not treat Hagar well, traditional readings find fault with Hagar and contemporary readers condemn Sarah for showing neither compassion nor solidarity.

The story begins as Sarah, who has not given birth, offers her Egyptian slave Hagar as her surrogate. Ancient Near Eastern texts from Assyrian Anatolia (1900 B.C.E.); from Nuzi in Syria (1600 B.C.E.); from Southern Babylonia (500 B.C.E.); and from Babylon (1900 B.C.E.) portray the same arrangement. As the laws of King Hammurabi of Babylon show, the wife's gift of a slave as her surrogate forestalls the husband's taking a second wife.

Neither Sarah nor Abraham nor the ancient texts obtain the slave's consent: Using another person's body as a surrogate for one's own is part of the fabric of slavery. The womb, like the muscles, could be utilized for the good of the master. So Sarah proposes to be "built-up" through the action of Hagar's womb; Abraham agrees and Hagar must comply.

But the plan goes awry. Hagar, who is supposed to be a neutral body, reacts: "her mistress is lessened in her eyes." This "womb with legs" is a person with her own viewpoint. She knows that she has something Sarah doesn't have—fertility—and she no longer considers Sarah's status exalted. Sarah's sharp indictment of Abraham—"My wrong is all on you . . . God will judge between you and me"—is, in a way, what feminists call a "click moment." She realizes that she has lost her status and can do nothing because her husband has authority over both of them. Abraham understands the power issue and restores her authority: "Your slave girl is in your hands." Neither Abraham nor Sarah ever calls Hagar by name—her personhood gets in the way of their plan.

Sarah wants to reassert her dominance, and as her last act in the story, she "oppresses" Hagar, she "degrades" her. The story never explains how she oppresses a slave, who, by definition, is oppressed. She may simply have ignored her pregnancy and treated her like an ordinary slave: Asking a pregnant slave concubine to draw water from the well would be oppression and degradation.

Once again Hagar reacts. Not wanting to be under Sarah's authority, she runs away. The story goes with her to the wilderness, the same wilderness where Elijah meets an angel. An angel addresses Hagar by name—"Hagar, slave of Sarah, where have you come from and where are you going?"—and she simply answers, "I am running away from Sarah." The reader feels the pathos of the oppressed slave, but the angel says: "Go back to your mistress and continue to be oppressed under her hand." An informed biblical reader, ancient or modern, may be bewildered. Ancient Near Eastern laws demand that a runaway slave be returned to its owner. But biblical law requires everyone to help a runaway slave escape its owner. Why should an angel place the laws of property over the freedom of persons?

Hagar's angel has a threefold message: "Return and be oppressed"; "I will multiply your seed so that it can't be counted"; "You are pregnant and you will give birth to a son and call his name Ishmael ('God hears') because God has heard your oppression, and your son will be a wild onager of a man." Hagar will have a glorious progeny who can never be subjugated if she voluntarily goes back to be exploited.

Some elements of the story ring bells. Hagar is an Egyptian slave. Egypt is the land where God had to rescue Sarah from the house of Pharaoh (Genesis 12); Sarah herself is a just-freed slave. Egypt is also the site of the future Exodus story that lies at the basis of Israel's self-understanding. The two words "slave" and "Egypt" together form the mantra of ancient Israel: "We were slaves in Egypt and God took us out of there." This mantra lies deep within Israel's consciousness. The story's identification of Hagar as an "Egyptian slave" is a direct allusion to the central myth of Israel's origins.

Another allusive detail: Sarah "degrades" Hagar in the same language used to describe the Egyptian treatment of their Israelite slaves in Israel's ancient creed: ". . . the Egyptians made us into slaves. And they oppressed us . . . and God heard our affliction and brought us out of there . . ." (Deuteronomy 26). Another parallel: The angel demands that Hagar return and be oppressed; in the previous chapter, God tells Abraham that his descendants will be strangers in a land that is not theirs, and the people will enslave and oppress them, before God will redeem them. And another: God hears Hagar's affliction and Israel's. And another: God promises both Abraham and Hagar multiple progeny.

The story of Hagar is the story of Israel, and their close correspondence continues. After the birth of Isaac, Abraham sends Hagar and Ishmael away. They are not sold; they are freed. They leave Abraham's household as emancipated slaves and wander thirsty in the desert until, miraculously, God gives them water and pronounces the great future of Ishmael. The emancipated Israelite slaves also wandered thirsty till God brought water to the desert (Exodus 15–18). In slavery and in freedom, Hagar is Israel.

The story of Sarah and Hagar is not a story of the conflict between "us" and "other," but between "us" and "another us." Hagar is the archetype of Israel: She is us. Sarah is both archetype and mother of Israel: She is both us and the one from whom we are born. This story forces us to realize that the destiny of Israel is not utterly different from that of the people around it. Ishmael's God-given destiny of utter freedom may have looked very attractive to an often marginal and exploited Israel on the brink of destruction.

The story raises ethical questions. Why does God insist that we suffer before we are rewarded? Israel has to wait its turn until the "iniquity of the Amorites is complete" (Genesis 15), but why does Israel have to become degraded slaves? Abraham's descendants have repeated this scenario many times. The idea that oppression is the path to redemption offers hope to those in the throes of calamity, but it is an unexplained aspect of God's behavior.

Sarah's behavior also disturbs us, for her experience as a slave does not make her more empathic to the slave in her home. It makes her want to assert her dominance so she won't lose it again. The story shows us how easily the oppressed can become oppressors.

We live in a world in which many peoples are experiencing their liberation. Once again the children of Hagar and the children of Sarah must work out their covenanted futures in relationship with each other. The issues raised by the Sarah–Hagar story play themselves out in our contemporary consciousness as we realize that a history of oppression does not guarantee that we cannot become oppressors and that the destiny of one nation is intricately intertwined with the destiny of others. The nuanced, non-triumphalist understanding of reality in Genesis can empower our own struggles.

––––––––––

Tikva Frymer-Kensky is Professor of Hebrew Bible at the University of Chicago Divinity School and the author of *In the Wake of the Goddesses: Women, Culture, and the Transformation of Pagan Myth* and *Motherprayer: The Pregnant Woman's Spiritual Companion*.

QUESTIONS

- Do you think that Abraham, Sarah, and Hagar could have worked things out in a better way for their families?

- What gives Hagar the strength to rebel? Do you think her rebellion makes her the heroine of the story?

✕~ ACTIVITIES FOR GROUPS AND FAMILIES

1) THE ART OF LEAVING (PART 2)

Look at the Rembrandt etching called *Dismissal of Hagar* (on page 103), which depicts the moment when Hagar and Ishmael leave Abraham (based

(continued on page 102)

WHO DO YOU IDENTIFY WITH IN THIS STORY—SARAH OR HAGAR?

My heart goes out to Hagar all the way. The arrangement was for Sarah's benefit. In the ancient Near East, if a sterile woman gave her husband a concubine for childbearing purposes, he was forbidden, by law, to take a mistress of his own. The system gave the wife a measure of control—and Sarah suggested it. Poor Hagar is caught up in some divine drama and then jettisoned, when she's played her part—chucked out into the wilderness with woefully inadequate provisions. In sending them away, Abraham sacrifices Ishmael as later he will almost sacrifice Isaac. Both children are brought to the point of death—though the Lord steps in at the eleventh hour.

> —**Karen Armstrong**, a series participant, is the author of *A History of God* and *In the Beginning: An Interpretation of the Book of Genesis*

For black women, the story of Hagar is a haunting one. It is a story of exploitation and persecution suffered by an Egyptian slave woman at the hands of her Hebrew mistress. Even if it is not our individual story, it is a story we have read in our mothers' eyes those afternoons when we greeted them at the front door after a hard day of work as a domestic. And if not our mothers' story, then it is certainly most of our grandmothers' story. For black women, Hagar's story is peculiarly familiar. It is as if we know it by heart . . . At some times in our lives, whether we are black or white, we are all Hagar's daughters. When our backs are up against a wall; when we feel abandoned, abused, betrayed, and banished; when we find ourselves in need of another woman's help . . . we, like Hagar, are in need of a woman who will "sister" us, not exploit us.

> —**Renita J. Weems**, a series participant, is a professor of Old Testament studies at Vanderbilt University Divinity School (from *Just a Sister Away*, 1988)

I identify with both Hagar and Sarah, although the sympathy for the maidservant comes more effortlessly. How can the reader not empathize with Hagar, especially as she's seen awaiting Ishmael's death in the wilderness? The text zooms in so closely on her in these verses, providing such a startlingly intimate picture of her hopelessness and sorrow. In contrast to Hagar's tragic passivity, Sarah acts, and what compels her actions is the fierceness of her passions surrounding motherhood. What makes Sarah a tragic figure is her desperation to control the future, and she becomes, to a certain extent and in true tragic fashion, the agent of her own downfall. She precipitates the birth of that very Ishmael whose existence she will come to feel threatens her own miracle-child Isaac—an unforeseen complication that might already have suggested to her the uncertainty of trying to force the future. But she's still at it when she banishes Hagar and Ishmael. She's a mother obsessed, seeking all and any possible dangers to her child so that she can remove them, childproof the future like a good parent childproofs the home. In the fierceness of her love she imagines that this is really possible. Soon after this comes Abraham's binding of Isaac, and with it Sarah learns—with a despair that's fatal, according to rabbinic tradition—the futility of her life's project.

—**Rebecca Goldstein**, a series participant, is the
author of *Mazel* and *The Mind-Body Problem*

In a sense, Sarah the banisher and Hagar the banished share the same fear. Though differently privileged and provided for, both are afraid that there won't be enough—not enough love to go around, not enough water to survive, not enough of an inheritance for two sons. The grace God offers is not primarily the provision of "more." Rather, divine grace affords the vision to discover, to create, and sometimes merely to notice sufficiency. "And God opened her eyes and she saw a well of water" (Genesis 21:18). So often, I find that what we request of God is already before us, within our grasp, granted long ago and with surfeit.

—**Rabbi Debra Orenstein**, a senior fellow
of the Wilstein Institute and instructor at the
University of Judaism in Los Angeles, is the
editor of *Lifecycles 1: Jewish Women on Life
Passages and Personal Milestones*

The language of the question "Do you identify with Sarah or Hagar?"—indeed the question itself—is all wrong. It expresses a vision seen through the eyes of a patriarch, a vision that has created great problems for women, that has encouraged them to turn against each other. All women bear the grief of the separation of Sarah and Hagar. The grief of the woman who fears she is not desired or desirable, that she is too old, infertile—not womanly. The fear of the desired, desirable woman that her body is her only currency and that, lacking protection of the law, she and hers are unsafe. How much better if Hagar and Sarah had embraced as sisters with the words: "We're in the same boat. The problem is, we're not steering it."

—**Mary Gordon**, a series participant, teaches English at Barnard College and is the author of *Final Payments*, *The Company of Women*, and *The Shadow Man*

If I were writing Sarah's music . . . Sarah is inside all of us; it's a question of finding her in me. With Sarah, what I find inside me is her silence, her waiting, her wisdom, her irony—after ninety years, her irony is almost bitter, but there is still hope. With Sarah, I wouldn't want to hear real tones. Her music is like a heartbeat . . . and tears dropping. You have the sense of a pulse, but an unpredictable one. It doesn't build, and you don't know how it will end. It just keeps going. In that softness, it's very determined.

—**Elizabeth Swados**, a series participant, is a writer and musician, most recently of *Bible Women* (from "Call and Promise" program)

I was born into a practicing Hindu family of the Brahmin caste . . . It is, of course, Hagar's story that haunts me. Hagar floats into my nightmares on work-toughened feet, and shrieks for a fairer representation for the disempowered and the abused. I urge Hagar not to take Sarah's afflicting of her too personally . . . We don't get Hagar's reaction to Sarah's plan of farming out her womb. Those of us who have experienced class prejudice and colonialism can be forgiven for reading into this omission the sad, silenced issues of disenfranchisement . . . Postmenopausal Sarah feels threatened as a woman [and] complains of Hagar's arrogance. If barren Sarah has imagined Hagar's slighting of her, her pain and her bitter defensiveness as a childless woman in a fertility-celebrating culture become endearingly believable. If the insult is real, Hagar is practicing dissent.

> —**Bharati Mukherjee**, a series participant, is a professor of English at the University of California at Berkeley and the author of *Jasmine* and *The Holder of the World* (from *Communion*, 1996)

The story of Hagar with Sarah is not mentioned in the Qur'an, but commentators tell us that Hagar was a stranger from Egypt in Abraham's household. She was powerless and dispossessed. Sarah, on the other hand, was living among her own people. Yet, though powerful, she was insecure because of her barrenness. I can identify with neither woman. They were both victims of a patriarchal society. I personally identify instead with the Queen of Sheba, a strong, capable, and intelligent leader who, according to the Qur'an, negotiated with King Solomon and consulted her people before taking major decisions.

> —**Azizah al-Hibri**, a series participant, is a professor of law at the University of Richmond

on Genesis 21:14). From the etching, what do you think each of the three is feeling? Who seems saddest? What other emotions do you see on their faces or in their body language?

2) BLESSED EVENTS

As a group, write Abraham and Sarah's birth announcement for Ishmael. Then write their birth announcement for Isaac.

3) CAN THIS FAMILY BE SAVED?

When you meet, ask a few group members to pretend to be part of a panel of experts on family dynamics on a TV talk show and ask another group member to act as moderator and take questions from the audience (the rest of the group members). Among the questions you might want the panel to answer: What would your advice to Abraham, Sarah, and Hagar be? Is it a good solution for Hagar and Ishmael to move away? Are there any other options, that is, alternatives that could resolve family tension without separating Ishmael and Isaac from one another? Assuming that separation is the best solution possible, what would you recommend in terms of visitation? Staying in touch? Imagine it is twenty years later: What do you think will have become of each member of the family if they decide to separate? If they decide to stay together?

4) EULOGIZING ABRAHAM

The Bible tells us that Ishmael and Isaac, together, buried their father, Abraham (Genesis 25:9). Divide the group and have one half write Ishmael's eulogy for Abraham and the other half write Isaac's eulogy. Then choose two people to deliver them to the whole group. Ask: How are the eulogies similar? How are they different? Which son had the better relationship with his father? Which son do you identify with?

✐ REFLECTIONS: ON MOTHERHOOD

All that I am, or hope to be, I owe to my angel mother.

—**Abraham Lincoln**

Rembrandt, *Dismissal of Hagar*. (From the Metropolitan Museum of Art, New York City; c. 1645. Reprinted with permission.)

Whatever else is unsure in this . . . world a mother's love is not.

> —**James Joyce,** *A Portrait of the Artist
> as a Young Man* (1916)

Sometimes when I look at all my children, I say to myself, "Lillian, you should have stayed a virgin."   —**Lillian Carter**

Having family responsibilities and concerns just has to make you a more understanding person.   —**Justice Sandra Day O'Connor**

A woman *is* her mother.
That's the main thing.   —**Anne Sexton,** *Housewife* (1962)

Parenthood has the power to redefine every aspect of life—marriage, work, relationships with family and friends. Those helpless bundles of power and promise that come into our world show us our true selves—who we are, who we are not, who we wish we could be.

> —**Hillary Rodham Clinton,** *It Takes a Village* (1995)

If you bungle raising your children, I don't think whatever else you do matters very much.   —**Jacqueline Kennedy Onassis**

A mother is not a person to lean on, but a person to make leaning unnecessary.   —**Dorothy Canfield Fisher,** *Her Son's Wife* (1926)

In search of my mother's garden, I found my own.

> —**Alice Walker,** *In Search of Our Mothers' Gardens*
> (1974)

If you have never been hated by your child, you have never been a parent.   —**Bette Davis,** *The Lonely Life* (1962)

He is Father. Even more, God is Mother, who does not want to harm us.   —**Pope John Paul I,** in St. Peter's Square,
September 17, 1978

Wynonna had her head on my right shoulder, and Ashley had her head on my left. I just felt this moment of exquisite completion. They are truly my other halves, the flesh of my flesh, the bone of my bone.   —**Naomi Judd**

7 THE TEST

✒ THE STORY OF ABRAHAM AND ISAAC ON MOUNT MORIAH: Genesis 22–23

And it happened after these things, that God tested Abraham and said unto him, "Abraham." And he replied, "Here I am." And He said, "Please take your son, your only one, whom you love—Isaac—and go to the land of Moriah; bring him up there as an offering upon one of the mountains which I shall tell you." (Genesis 22:1–2, *The Chumash: The Stone Edition/Artscroll*)

The story of Abraham and Isaac on Mount Moriah is "the molten core of the patriarchal tradition," Peter Pitzele has written, "a nightmare place where Imagination conceives its ultimate ordeal." It is such a powerful story that it is hard to believe that it occupies only nineteen verses in the biblical narrative. In the same distinctive language with which God initially called Abraham to leave his home ("*Lech lecha*": "Go forth"), this story opens with God again commanding Abraham to "go forth," this time to sacrifice Isaac. If, with the first call, God was asking Abraham to give up his past, with this call, God is asking him to give up his future, his son. In this sense, Abraham's saga comes full circle, and his role on the biblical stage comes to an end. Although Abraham will live for many more years, as far as we know, God never speaks to him again.

In the thousands of years since it was written, Christians, Jews, and Muslims have all struggled with this story, and the story of the sacrificial son has been central to all three traditions. Not surprisingly, though, Christians, Jews, and Muslims have interpreted the story in very different ways, even naming it differently. For Christians, it has been the sacrifice of Isaac, prefiguring another Father's sacrifice of another son, in whose death-that-was-not-death Christianity was founded. For Jews, it is the *Akedah* or the binding of Isaac, with the son's response to his ordeal representing the people of Israel's response to their ordeals. Like the Jews, Isaac did not choose his fate but was chosen; nonetheless, his faith in and obedience to God, like his father Abraham's, remain steadfast. Although the Qur'an never specifies, most Muslim commentaries say that it was Ishmael whom Abraham took to Moriah, and the willingness of both father and son to submit to Allah's will—Ishmael is a fully comprehending partner in the Islamic version of the drama—is seen by Muslims as the highest, most admirable form of faith. (The word "Muslim" is derived from the Arabic for "willingness to submit to Allah.") Even though they have read the story in different ways, all three faiths agree that this story raises some of the most difficult questions ever posed by and to humankind.

Now read the story of God's command to Abraham and Abraham and Isaac's journey to Mount Moriah in your Bible. As you do, consider the following questions:

- Why does God test humans? Especially one as faithful as Abraham has already shown himself to be?

- What exactly is the test here? Is it a test of Abraham's absolute and unquestioning faith and obedience or is it a test of man's willingness to challenge God?

- How would you describe Abraham's faith? How does it compare to Isaac's? To your own?

- Where was Sarah? What might be different about this story if God had commanded Sarah to sacrifice Isaac?

- Do you think it will ever be possible for Isaac to forgive his father? To forgive God?

- Why does this story make us so uncomfortable today?

- Do you believe that God always requires that we sacrifice (or be willing to sacrifice) what we love most?

SACRIFICE
by Reverend Lawrence Boadt

In this essay, Reverend Lawrence Boadt discusses questions that have been raised over the centuries about the story of the sacrifice of Isaac. Ultimately, Boadt says, because God's goodness is manifest in ways beyond our comprehension, the most important thing is to trust in and hold faith with God. He urges all of us to consider what the story can tell us about humankind's never-ending struggle to understand the nature of God, how faith works, and the coexistence of good and evil in our world.

All biblical stories carry a wealth of meaning. But no story perhaps has so gripped the imagination of readers over the centuries as the terrifying proposition of Genesis 22 that God would ask a faithful person to kill his own son to prove his love for God. Certainly no other person in the Book of Genesis ever encounters such a poignant and heart-wrenching experience as this.

Scholars and spiritual writers have often suggested that the story was originally intended to explain how God forbade the practice of human sacrifice or how the mountain to which Abraham went was the same Mount Moriah on which the temple later stood. The text focuses on a specific challenge: God wanted to see if Abraham would obey no matter what in order to reconfirm the promises and blessings for his descendants. But many other ways of reading are possible.

Note its simple narrative technique. The story wastes no words on the background or even on the feelings of those involved. It is one of the most tautly written and emotionally charged masterpieces in world literature precisely because of what it doesn't say. It begins starkly: God will test Abraham. No reason is given and Abraham never asks for one. In earlier chapters, Abraham has always followed wherever God led him. Even now he stands ready: Three times, he simply says, "Here I am" (vv. 1, 7, 11). The plot itself emphasizes traveling distances and the objects needed for a sacrifice. Spaced between these are four brief conversations. With just a few words per stage, the drama moves relentlessly forward. The reader must fill in the gaps both from the imagination and from information provided in the previous chapter.

As a result, suspense is created at every stage in the action of the plot, but also in the reader's mind: Why does God test humans? Since the story opens with a clear claim that God is testing Abraham, what will the drama say about a God who does this? If Abraham has already proved faithful time and again, does God never allow a final "okay" to our human obedience? Is there an insight here into the mystery of the relationship between God and humanity that always remains ambivalent and difficult for us to comprehend? We live with ignorance, imperfection, evil, and mortality, while God has usually been viewed without any of these limitations. Does this encounter underscore the impossibility of understanding God? Does it suggest that God is not fully aware or in control of our destinies? If God is still unsure of Abraham, does this become a story of hope for all of us for whom God sometimes seems alien or distant or silent?

What about God as Good? God not only asks for a test, but that test involves a sacrifice. Is there any difference between "sacrificing" your son and "murdering" him? Are we asked to do evil to please God?

If it is only a test, we should not get trapped by feelings of horror and dismay that God would order such a cruel act. Like children asking for the story of *Little Red Riding Hood* or *Goldilocks and the Three Bears*, every reader knows the outcome of the test before actually reading it. Many children learned it—one of the best-known biblical stories—at their mother's knee. They saw it as a game—it is a test, only a test, whose outcome is certain.

But what if it is not intended as a test? Perhaps Abraham has been too successful, perhaps his obedience is the obedience that Satan accuses Job of having: he obeys because he always received blessing as a result. God does say at the climax in verse 12, "Now I know you fear God" (*New Revised Standard Version*), or perhaps better, "Now I know you stand in awe of God." Is this really a story about the difficulty of human submission to God at all costs?

Is there a positive message of trust? Since the "test" revolves around the fundamental question of fidelity—God's as well as Abraham's—we can also read the bottom line of the drama, with its favorable outcome and its renewed promise of blessing, as an affirmation in the face of despair or disaster of God, who is both present to us and "provides" for us (v. 8) what we need. God's goodness is manifest in ways beyond our comprehension, but in this dilemma, nothing is more important than trusting and holding faith with the God we have come to know through revelation and experience, just as Abraham had in the preceding stories.

At the end, the sacrifice of Isaac is both a story of how faith works and how our experience copes with good and evil in life. We find both blessing and testing in our relationship with God, but the divine/human dialogue never ceases.

Reverend Lawrence Boadt, C.S.P., is a professor of biblical studies at the Washington Theological Union, a Roman Catholic graduate school in Washington, D.C. A senior editor at the Paulist Press, he is the author of *Reading the Old Testament*.

QUESTIONS

- Why did God command Abraham to sacrifice Isaac? Why did He, at the last moment, still Abraham's hand?

- Does this story affirm your faith in God's goodness?

ARGUING WITH GOD
by Rosann Catalano

Over the centuries, countless explanations have been offered for Abraham's failure to argue with God on Mount Moriah. Perhaps he knew that it was only a test. Perhaps he was a zealot whose love of God superceded all family ties. Perhaps he was still resentful over Ishmael and so the sacrifice of Isaac was not so difficult for him. Perhaps he had become disheartened by God's many tests. Perhaps he had come to believe that arguing with God was futile, that the best man could do was to learn what God's plan was—and in this case, he did not want to know what God's plan was. Perhaps he felt that arguing on behalf of others was part of our obligation to pursue justice, but that arguing on his own behalf was self-serving.

Perhaps he understood that God, in every age, asks us to demonstrate our faith by giving up what is most important to us. Perhaps . . .

════════
⤙⚒⤚

While the notion of arguing with God may strike some as outrageous or blasphemous, it is part of the larger lament tradition that is deeply embedded in both the Hebrew Bible and the Christian Testament. The laments of Moses, Samson, Rebekah, Elijah, Jeremiah, Job, and Jesus all belong to this tradition, one which has profound implications for the ways in which Jews and Christians understand both the character of God and the nature of their relationship with God.

The lament tradition rises out of the anguish experienced when the hopes and claims of faith come into direct conflict with the reality of human suffering. Here is prayer which disregards all pretense and politeness by issuing a bold protest that appeals to God to alter the situation. Laced with the language of expectation, this is a tradition that storms the gates of heaven in search of the God who promised to be a God of compassion and mercy.

In Genesis 18, Abraham argues with God against the decision to destroy Sodom and Gomorrah. That God accedes to the temerity and tenacity of Abraham witnesses both to the persuasive power of the lament and to the willingness of God to be moved by the prayer of those created in God's own image.

Against the backdrop of this tradition, what are we to make of Abraham's silence when God demands that he sacrifice his son, Isaac? Perhaps it is beyond us to discern God's will, but surely we are required to wrestle with Abraham's response. Four chapters earlier, he presses God again and again for the sake of the righteous of Sodom and Gomorrah whom he does not know; but now in the face of this scandalous demand, he remains silent. What are we to make of Abraham's docility and his blind obedience to God? Given the tragic history of the twentieth century, is this model of submissive faith one we want to encourage in our own time?

───────────

Rosann Catalano is Theologian-in-Residence at the Institute for Christian and Jewish Studies and an adjunct professor at St. Mary's Seminary in Baltimore.

QUESTIONS

- What do you think you would have done in Abraham's place? Would you have argued or pleaded with God? In what ways do you argue with God now?

WHERE WAS SARAH?
by Phyllis Trible

Attachment threatened the obedience, the worship, the fear of God . . . Nowhere prior to Genesis 22 does Abraham emerge as a man of attachment. That is not his problem . . .

Attachment *is* Sarah's problem. Nevertheless, Genesis 22 drops Sarah to insert Abraham. The switch defies the internal logic of the larger story. In view of the unique status of Sarah and her exclusive relationship to Isaac, she, not Abraham, ought to have been tested. The dynamic of the entire saga, from its genealogical preface on, requires that Sarah be featured in the climactic scene, that she learn the meaning of obedience to God, that she find liberation from possessiveness, that she free Isaac from maternal ties, and that she emerge a solitary individual, nonattached, the model of faithfulness. In making Abraham the object of the divine test, the story violates its own rhythm and movement. Moreover, it fails to offer Sarah redemption and thereby perpetuates the conflict between her and Hagar . . .

Patriarchy has denied Sarah her story, the opportunity for freedom and blessing. It has excluded her and glorified Abraham. And it has not stopped with these things. After securing the safety of Isaac, it has no more need for Sarah; so it moves to eliminate her.

Phyllis Trible, a series participant, is a professor of sacred literature at Union Theological Seminary in New York City and author of *Texts of Terror: Literary Feminist Readings of Biblical Narratives*. This piece is excerpted from "Genesis 22: The Sacrifice of Sarah," in *Not in Heaven: Coherence and Complexity in Biblical Narrative*, edited by Jason Rosenblatt and Joseph Sitterson (1991).

ISAAC—VICTIM OR MARTYR?

Instead of Isaac, the righteous son, a ram appeared to be the victim, so that Isaac might be released from his bonds. Sacrificing the ram, Abraham released Isaac just as the Lord [Jesus Christ] becoming a victim released us. Being bound he released; and being sacrificed he redeemed. For the Lord was a lamb, just like the ram Abraham saw tethered in the bush of Sabek. Truly the bush represents the cross, that place in Jerusalem, and the lamb is the Lord, bound for sacrifice.

—**Melito of Sardis** (ca. 180)

Abraham stretched out his hand and took a knife to kill Isaac his son. Isaac answered and said to his father: Bind my hands properly that I may not struggle in the time of my pain and disturb you and render your offering unfit and be cast into the pit of destruction in the world to come. The eyes of Abraham were turned to the eyes of Isaac, but the eyes of Isaac were turned to the angels in heaven. Isaac saw them but Abraham did not see them. In that hour the angels in heaven (a heavenly voice) went out and said to each other: Let us go and see the only two just men in the world. The one slays, and the other is being slain. The slayer does not hesitate and the one being slain stretches out his neck.

—**Fragmentary Targum**, Second century Aramaic text

We are all like Abraham; so involved in our outside world—our careers, interests, or principles—that we do not or cannot see that it is our child, or spouse or parent that is bound on the altar. We are so adept at sacrificing that which is truly important to us on the altars we have erected that we may ask whether we are capable of hearing the cry of the angel before it's too late.

—**Rabbi Norman Cohen**, a series participant,
from *Self, Struggle, and Change* (1995)

Like father, like son. Isaac is neither victim nor martyr, but protagonist, challenging his father as his father challenged God, and it is with Isaac that we wait in breathless suspense to find out, will Abraham pass the test? And then—at last!—the denouement, the famous ram. There is death at Moriah, but it is a *symbolic* death, one that reconciles father and son, one that defines the God of the Jews.

Thousands of years after the patriarchs of Israel, a Jew in Vienna read Oedipus, and so doing, found a new, deeply mystical metaphor to explain Abraham's ram. The resolution of an infant's primary psychic conflict with his father, Freud showed, is not a murderous act but an act of symbolization: the child begins to learn to symbolize desire in speech. Oedipal desire is not carried out, no more than Abraham carried out his sacrifice of his son, nor is it resolved, but is expressed and reconciled in that ultimate symbolic structure, language.

—**Neil Gordon**, author of *The Sacrifice of Isaac*

He [Abraham] said: "Grant me a son, Lord, and let him be a righteous man." We gave him news of a gentle son. And when he reached the age when he could work with him his father said to him: "My son, I dreamt that I was sacrificing you. Tell me what you think." He replied: "Father, do as you are bidden. Allah willing, you shall find me faithful." And when they had both surrendered themselves to Allah's will, and Abraham had laid his son prostrate upon his face, We called out to him, saying: "Abraham, you have fulfilled your vision." Thus did We reward the righteous. That was indeed a bitter test. We ransomed his son with a noble sacrifice and bestowed on him the praise of later generations. "Peace be on Abraham."   —**Qur'an, Surah XXXVII, 100–109**

Is the relationship with the deity one in which the people of God can expect to be put to the test again and again? Are there absurd, senseless experiences in life that can become the occasion to turn away from God? There may well be a deep, dark, and seemingly hopeless valley through which we travel . . . We should learn from this story that receiving promises does not entail being protected from moments where those promises seem to be called into question.   —**Terence Fretheim**, *The New Interpreter's Bible* (1994)

ACTIVITIES FOR GROUPS AND FAMILIES

1) READING THE TEXT: ABRAHAM'S TESTS

In Hebrew, the language of God's command to Abraham to take his son Isaac and "go forth" ("Lech lecha") to the land of Moriah (Genesis 22:2) is precisely the same as the language God used to call Abraham initially from his father's house (Genesis 12:1). As a group, look first at Chapter 12, then at Chapter 22, and chart what Abraham and the others did in each story. Then, compare the blessings they ultimately received (see Genesis 12:7 and Genesis 22:17). Consider: How is God testing Abraham in each story? What do these two tests have in common? What seem to be the risks and rewards for Abraham in each story? Have God's commands become harder or easier for Abraham to obey as time has passed and he has aged? Does this make sense to you in light of your own experiences?

2) THE ART OF SACRIFICE

In her book *Handmade Midrash,* Jo Milgrom has created an activity to help give us a personal, emotional understanding of this difficult story. For the group to do this activity, you will need a few sheets of colored construction paper for each person, and tape or glue.

As a group, first review the story of the sacrifice/binding of Isaac in Genesis 22. Then have each person first tear construction paper into five shapes representing Abraham, Isaac, the ram, the altar, and God. Ask people to glue the shapes to a blank piece of paper in an arrangement that best represents their vision of the relationships between these five "characters" in the story. Work in silence. When you have all finished, go around the circle and ask each person to talk about his/her picture, explaining why s/he chose those particular colors and shapes and what the relationship among the shapes means to him/her. When you describe your picture to the group, think about: What does your picture say about relationships between parents and children? Between God and humans? Does your picture accurately convey your feelings and thoughts about the story? If you were to do it over again, what, if anything, would you change? What, if anything, can your finished picture add to your under-standing of the story?

3) IMAGINING: ON MOUNT MORIAH

Assign various group members to play Abraham, Isaac, the two servants who accompany them to Moriah, and Sarah. Reenact the scene the way you imagine it happened, beginning with Abraham and Isaac leaving home and ending when Sarah hears the story of what happened. Afterward, have the people who participated in the reenactment stay in role so that the group can question them. For example, the group might want to ask of Abraham: Why didn't you refuse, or at least protest and argue? Can you find the words to explain to us why you kept silent, why you seemingly obeyed God so willingly? Ask of Isaac: Did you submit willingly? When did you know what was going to happen—or did you not know until it was actually happening? Now, afterward, what do you feel? How do you feel about your father? About God? Will there be lasting repercussions of this event for you? Ask of Sarah: Did you believe Abraham about where he said he and Isaac were going when they left home that morning? Do you now know where Abraham took him? Who told you? If you suspected what was going to happen, why did you let them go? What do you think you would have done if God had asked of you what God asked of Abraham?

⌦ REFLECTIONS: ON SACRIFICE

Too long a sacrifice
Can make a stone of the heart.

—**William Butler Yeats**, *Easter 1916* (1921)

The sacrifices of friendship were beautiful in her eyes as long as she was not asked to make them.

—**Saki (H. H. Munro)**, *Beasts and Super-Beasts* (1914)

Nothing so much enhances a good as to make sacrifices for it.

—**George Santayana**, *The Sense of Beauty* (1896)

Sacrificers are not the ones to pity. The ones to pity are those they sacrifice.

> —**Elizabeth Bowen**, *The Death of the Heart* (1938)

To die for a religion is easier than to live it absolutely.

> —**Jorge Luis Borges**, *Labyrinths* (1962)

To love is to know the sacrifices which eternity exacts from life.

> —**Pearl Craigie**, *Schools of Saints* (1897)

A man must be sacrificed now and again
To provide for the next generation of men.

> —**Amy Lowell**, *A Critical Fable* (1922)

I have sacrificed everything in my life that I consider precious in order to advance the political career of my husband.

> —**Pat Nixon**, quoted in *Women at Work*, by Betty Medsger (1975)

There are events without which one's life becomes unimportant, a worthless toy; and there are times when one is commanded to do something, even at the price of one's life.

> —**Hannah Senesh**, in her diary, December 25, 1943

To gain that which is worth having, it may be necessary to lose everything else.

> —**Bernadette Devlin**, *The Price of My Soul* (1969)

Greater love hath no man than this, that a man lay down his life for his friends.

> —**John 15:13**, New Testament.

For the sake of a family an individual may be sacrificed; for the sake of a village a family may be sacrificed; for the sake of a nation a village may be sacrificed; for the sake of one's self the world may be sacrificed.

—**Panchatantra** (ca. fifth century)

Ye will not attain unto piety until ye spend of that which ye love. And whatsoever ye spend, God is aware thereof.

—**Qur'an, Surah III, 92**

8 BLESSED DECEPTION

⤫ THE STORY OF ISAAC, REBEKAH, ESAU, AND JACOB: GENESIS 25–28

Isaac prayed to the Lord on behalf of his wife, because she was barren. The Lord answered his prayer, and his wife Rebekah became pregnant. The babies jostled within her . . . [s]o she went to inquire of the Lord. The Lord said to her, "Two nations are in your womb, and two peoples from within you will be separated; one people will be stronger than the other, and the older will serve the younger." When the time came for her to give birth, there were twin boys in her womb. The first to come out was red, and his whole body was like a hairy garment, so they named him Esau [hairy]. After this, his brother came out, with his hand grasping Esau's heel, so he was named Jacob [he grasps the heels, or he deceives]. (Genesis 25:21–26, *New International Version*)

Isaac, Rebekah, Esau, and Jacob—they are one of the most difficult families to understand in the whole of the Bible. Just stop for a moment and consider: Esau and Jacob are twins, but they don't look or act like twins—or even like brothers. By the end of this part of the story, Jacob has deceived Esau, stolen both his birthright and their father's blessing, and has fled; Esau, in turn, has sworn to find and kill Jacob. More than twenty years will pass before they see one another again.

And Isaac and Rebekah, parents who quite openly play favorites with their children, are a husband and a wife who don't communicate with each other. Isaac seems never to have recovered from the trauma he suffered at his own father's hand on Mount Moriah. Rebekah, chosen for Isaac by Abraham, is clearly stronger than her husband: Is there anything she can't or won't do? Even before she gives birth to the twins, she has the distinction of being the first woman in the Bible to speak to God and get a direct answer. After the boys' birth, she determines to secure God and Isaac's blessing for her favored son, Jacob, no matter what the obstacles or cost.

But all families are more than their individual members, and their stories are more than their individual actions. Everything that each person does affects the others, changes the family balance. Maybe Rebekah is so strong because Isaac is weak. Maybe Jacob and Esau are not total opposites, defined only in opposition to one another. Ultimately, these brothers will only be able to come to terms with themselves when they are able to see how "the other" lives within them, too.

Now read the story of Isaac, Rebekah, Esau, and Jacob in your Bible. As you do, consider the following questions:

- How is Rebekah's relationship with God different from those of the women who preceded her in Genesis?

- What is so important about blessing, whether from Isaac or from God? Can a blessing be shared?

- What motivates Rebekah?

- Is deception ever warranted?

- Why is brotherhood so difficult between brothers?

SIBLING RIVALRY, REDUX: JACOB AND ESAU
by Noam Zion

In his essay, Noam Zion discusses the "uses and abuses" of twins, the dream and the failures of brotherhood, not only in Genesis, but in our own time. An American Jew who moved to Israel more than twenty years ago, Zion sees Esau and Jacob's struggle writ large in the world today.

The "brotherhood of man" is surely one of the most enduring dreams of the soul. We do not find even a hint of that
dream in the myths of the Greeks or in the folk traditions of
Europe, but it is one of the central conceptions of the Bible.
What that book makes clear . . . is how vexed such a brotherhood really is, what distances, differences, inequities, and
fears must be overcome and accepted before we will be able
to live in peace with one another.

—**Peter Pitzele**, *Our Fathers' Wells* (1995)

If all humans are brothers, sharing a common identity, then
twins should represent the ultimate of brotherhood. Yet, too
often, twins can be adversarial siblings, whose blood ties seem no
more than a passing biological accident. In the story of the first
twins in the Bible, Jacob and Esau, the notion of brotherhood goes
awry. Jacob, the younger twin, displaces his older brother Esau,
usurping his birthright twice—buying it for lentil soup and stealing it from their blind father. Over the centuries, the heirs of
Jacob—both Jewish and Christian—have used this story to support their devaluation of their own so-called brothers.

Rebekah, whose life mission is to guarantee her preferred
younger son's supremacy, uses whatever means are at hand to
fulfill God's private prophecy of Jacob's predominance. In fact,
God and Rebekah become allies driving a wedge of election and
destiny between the twins. Isaac, the blind, doting father who
loved Esau too well, is outmaneuvered; Esau, who sells his birthright for a pot of porridge, is disinherited. His sobbing plea that
he too might receive a blessing is heeded only with much delay
and in the most superficial sense.

The very notion of chosenness—one sibling chosen over another to receive the divine blessing—creates a tension with the
ideal of brotherhood, for choosing one implies that the other is
rejected; a hierarchy of winner and loser, master and slave, is created.

Just as Jacob successfully diverts the blessing for his benefit,
many "descendants" of Jacob have used the story to justify their
triumphalism over contemporary rivals. In ancient Israel, it was
the biological children of Jacob who claimed priority of blessing
and of land over Abraham's less favored posterity—Ishmael, fa-

ther of the Arabs; Lot, father of Moab and Amon (hence today's Amman, capital of Jordan); and especially Esau, father of the Edomites and the Amalekites. The Jews read a thousand years of acrimonious relations with their Semitic neighbor, Edom, into the sibling rivalry of Jacob and Esau.

In the era of the New Testament, the Christians discovered God's inscrutable grace in the choice of the younger son, Jacob, who represented the Church, over the elder Esau, the Synagogue. For the Church Fathers, election was determined not by birth order, not even by observance of the law, but by divine grace granted through Jesus Christ. According to this view, grace is given freely to the chosen one without regard to merit or sin; anyone can be called and saved or passed over and condemned.

In the rabbinic world, from the third century on, Esau's Edom came to be a code word for the Romans, who burned the Temple and exiled the Jews. Esau's hairy arms and hunting prowess matched the martial virtues of the Roman Empire and its love of gladiators. When Rome became Christianized, a thousand years of Christian persecution of Israel were read into Esau's temporary subjugation of Jacob in the Bible. According to this rabbinic reading, Israel, the descendants of Jacob, will ultimately unseat the rule of Esau: God's prophecy will come true when Rome is in ruins and Jerusalem is rebuilt.

These triumphalist readings of Jacob and Esau systematically suppress the common brotherhood of Israel and Edom, of the Church and the Synagogue. Such interpretations serve deep psychological as well as political needs, reassuring the underdog of moral superiority and the ultimate reversal of his fate. However, they also brutalize sibling relations, turning the brother into the "other," the twin into the mortal enemy.

However, an alternative reading of these biblical twins is available just below the surface in Genesis and in rabbinic tradition. We still may recapture much of the original sensitivity in Genesis to the pain of the brother and the ultimate hope for reconciliation. Truth be told, in Genesis, Jacob the younger never rules Esau the older. The stolen blessing of supremacy won by Rebekah and Jacob's deception is never consummated. Rather, it inaugurates twenty years of flight, exile, and servitude for Jacob and loneliness for Rebekah, who never again sees her favorite son: The clear lesson is that those who live by deception suffer by deception.

Even today, the narrator's account of Esau and Isaac's pain upon discovering the betrayal often evokes guilt and shame among the children of Israel, who read the story annually. Some of the rabbis explain Jacob's subsequent exile and Israel's exile under Roman rule as a just punishment, teaching all of us how it feels to be victims.

Millennia after the struggles of Jacob and Esau, each of us still claims to be the most beloved of God; we are each still in pursuit of the same patrimony of land, legitimacy, supremacy, and blessing. In the stories of siblings, Genesis offers to ancient and modern Israel a model for understanding its ongoing life-and-death struggles; the family feud offers a hopeful yet realistic image for these conflicts. Arabs and Jews are brothers sharing the same ancestors and the same humanity—we are all in the image of God. However, these brothers are not engaged merely in turf battles to be solved by pragmatic, diplomatic compromises and cleverly redrawn borders, but in issues of identity and dignity. We must work and pray for reconciliation or, at least, coexistence; my brother should not be demonized, but neither may I discount the possibility of fratricide. Idealism and realism must go hand in hand.

As siblings emphasize their differences, brotherhood breeds the deepest injuries to our relationships. A twin birth may divide the family into competing alliances—mother love arrayed against paternal preferences. But perhaps the problem and the solution are deeply intertwined. The birth of "fraternal twins" ironically bears witness to the possibility of enormous differences in character and physique of those born of the same womb. The recognition and respect of differences also hold out the hope of reconciliation—when brothers accept their disparate fates, when each goes off to his own land and his own lifestyle—when they realize that they do not want to be the other but to be themselves. Partition without the predominance of one over the other, geographic separation into independent clans, is the Genesis solution for Lot and Abraham, Ishmael and Isaac, Laban and Jacob, and finally Esau and Jacob.

For me personally as an American Jew and then as an Israeli, my initial inquiry into Christianity and Islam terrified me, for I discovered that historically these two sibling religions wanted to displace me—the firstborn, the first chosen one. In interfaith dialogue with my American-Christian colleagues around Genesis, we've come to understand that we need not displace one another. My fragile hope is that a similar process can and will occur with the Palestinian Muslims with whom I share the promised land. I hope that Jews, Christians, and Muslims will come to echo the words of Esau: "I have enough, my brother, let what is yours remain yours" (Genesis 33:9). When Christians stop dreaming of Jewish conversion to Christianity, and Muslims and Jews stop dreaming of exclusive control of Abraham's blessing, then there will be hope for mutual recognition among siblings. When all the biological and spiritual descendants of Abraham, Sarah, and Hagar learn that the pain of our brothers and sisters cannot be taken lightly—even when we believe divine destiny is on our side—then reconciliation may become a real possibility.

Noam Zion is on the faculty of the Shalom Hartman Institute of Jerusalem, and is the author of the forthcoming *The Family Participation Haggadah: A Different Night* (1997)

QUESTION

- What promise do you see for all the descendants of Jacob and Esau overcoming their differences as we near the twenty-first century?

REBEKAH, A TRICKSTER HEROINE
by Susan Niditch

In Genesis 27, Rebekah is the trickster who formulates the plan and succeeds, moving the men around her like chess pieces. Lest the reader think that here one finally encounters a more liberated woman, beware that again success is gained through the symbolic counterpart of sex: food. Moreover, the status in question is not that of the woman but of her son. Nevertheless, within the confines and assumptions of her male-dominated world, Rebekah is very good at what she does. Indeed, she determines and directs the course of the clan and in doing so is the one who knows and fulfills what God wants . . .

Rebekah's wisdom . . . is a vicarious power that achieves success for oneself through the success of male children, a power symbolically grounded in the preparation and serving of food. It involves as well a willingness to sacrifice oneself ("Let your curse be on me," 27:13) if necessary for the sake of the son. Such is woman's power in a man's world . . . It is the power of those not in authority. The woman in ancient Israelite literature who would succeed almost must be a trickster . . . Yet so clever is this trickster . . . so completely superior in wisdom to the men around her that she seems to be the creation of a woman storyteller, one who . . . subverts its (male-centered) rules indirectly by making Rebekah a trickster heroine, for this is also woman's power in a man's world, a power of mockery, humor, and deception.

Susan Niditch is the Samuel Green Professor of Religion at Amherst College and the author of *Underdogs and Tricksters: A Prelude to Biblical Folklore*. This piece is excerpted from *The Women's Commentary on the Bible*, edited by Carol Newsom and Sharon Ringe (1992).

QUESTIONS

- Do you see Rebekah as trickster? A heroine? Both?

- In this case, do you think the ends justified the means? Do the ends ever justify the means?

ACTIVITIES FOR GROUPS AND FAMILIES

1) READING THE TEXT: JACOB AND ESAU

In your group, read Genesis 25:23–34 aloud and then have people identify at least five ways that Jacob and Esau are different that might have caused conflict between the brothers while they were growing up. (Think about: physical traits, the work they do, parental attachments and preferences, linguistic and intellectual abilities, personalities.) On one side of a big piece of paper, write down the characteristics you identify as Esau's; on the other side, write down Jacob's. What are the different definitions of manhood

WHAT IS THE NATURE OF ISAAC'S BLINDNESS?

Now when Isaac was old and his eyes were too dim to see . . .
(Genesis 27:1, *The Jewish Publication Society Torah*)

Of all the patriarchs, Isaac receives the least attention. "He remains always a shadowy figure, obscure and incomplete," scholar Adin Steinsaltz has written. The silence that surrounds him suggests that he never recovered from the trauma of the events on Mount Moriah. Rabbinic interpretations in particular pay particular attention to the origin and meaning of Isaac's loss of sight.

When Isaac lay upon the altar, about to be sacrificed by his father, the angels wept, and their tears fell upon his eyes, and there they remained and weakened his sight.

—**Midrash Rabbah**

Isaac's blindness had to have been willful. Isaac, who had seen all too clearly the results of his father's "vision," chose, when his turn came, to "close his eyes" to Esau's intermarriage (Genesis 26:34–35), despite the pain it caused him. He refused to cut off the child who loved him.

—**Noam Zion**

R. Eleazar ben Azariah taught: From seeing the evil deeds of wicked Esau. For the Holy One said: "Shall Isaac go out into the marketplace and hear people say, 'This is that scoundrel's father'? I shall therefore dim Isaac's eyes so that he will stay home."

Or the phrase "from seeing" is to be explained by the tale of a distinguished man who had a beautiful and well-appointed reception room, next to which his neighbors used to burn stubble and straw, sending smoke in through the window. The man felt constrained to seal the window. Likewise, while Esau's wives worshipped idols, Isaac saw them and was so greatly distressed that at once his eyes grew dim.

—**Genesis Rabbah 65:10**

The image of Isaac's blindness reminds us that God is in control, not we ourselves. Out of circumstances that seem wrong to us, God can and does bring into being the good He wishes. His ways are not our ways; we have to keep learning and relearning that. What might seem to us a lack of justice would presuppose that we had rights to God's love and grace, and this is a way of saying: Not so.

—**Rembert Weakland, O.S.B.,**
Archbishop of Milwaukee

It was a blindness that left Isaac in darkness deeper than that which plagued Egypt. Isaac, who as a youth was blind to his half-brother's designs, who as he grew was blind to his father's dangerous devotion to God, who as he married was blind to the corruptions of his brother-in-law, who as he fathered was blind to the petty flatteries of his sons, who as he aged was blind to his wife's preference of one son and her schemes to advance him over the other—truly Isaac could not see. It was a total blindness, as only angel tears can bring.

—**Rabbi Burton L. Visotzky,** a series participant, from
Reading the Book (1991)

Isaac was said to have been blinded not only by the flames of the sacrifice of which he was almost a part, but by the *Shekhinah* [the divine presence] that appeared to him on that occasion. Some types of darkness and blindness are indicative of an excess of light.

—**Freema Gottlieb,** *The Lamp of God:*
A Jewish Book of Light (1989)

that emerge from these different characteristics? Are there similar points of difference and conflict in your own family? Are you and your brothers and sisters alike? How do your personal experiences shape your sympathy and antipathy toward Esau and/or Jacob? Have one group member play Esau and another play Jacob: Place them in a few situations and listen to them talk to one another. What can you learn from listening to the brothers this way?

2) WRITING AN ETHICAL WILL

An ethical will is a letter some of us choose to write, usually to our children, but also, on occasion, to our parents, our spouses, our siblings, and/or our friends to let them know our thoughts, hopes, and wishes for them, and to share with them (and also with ourselves) our strongest, most fundamental beliefs, the ones that we hope will survive us. Isaac's blessing of his sons (Genesis 27–28) and Jacob's blessing of his sons and grandsons (Genesis 49) could be seen as the precursors of ethical wills.

During the week before you meet, have each individual outline or write an ethical will, stating his/her principles and values to the next generation. (Think about: lessons you have learned, advice you might give, hard-won wisdom you want to share.) Then, when you meet, share your writing with the others and see if you are able to find any common principles and values that you all feel are important to pass on.

3) IMAGINING: REBEKAH'S STORY

Imagine yourself as Rebekah: You have just helped Jacob to disguise himself as Esau and sent him to Isaac to try to secure the blessing. Have group members take turns speaking as Rebekah. Ask her to justify her actions and tell the group what she expects to happen to each of her sons. What worries her most? What will make her happiest? What is securing the blessing worth to her?

As you listen to Rebekah, consider: Is Rebekah just trying to ensure that God's will, disclosed to her while she was pregnant, be done? Is she an overbearing and manipulative mother? Does having to choose between her two sons cause her pain? What do you imagine Rebekah and Isaac's relationship is like? Is deception ever warranted? Can you imagine situations in your own life where you might choose to deceive someone as Rebekah and Jacob deceived Isaac?

4) IMAGINING: ISAAC AND ESAU'S STORY

Imagine that you are Isaac. After you have given the blessing to Jacob, you find that you want to tell Esau why he has always been your favorite son and also why you mistakenly (?) gave the blessing to Jacob. How do you make sense of your inability to distinguish Jacob from Esau when they are so different? Because you are blind, it's clear why the evidence of your hands was more important than the evidence of your eyes. But why was it more important than the evidence of your ears, of hearing Jacob's voice? Ask one person to start the story in Isaac's voice and then go around the room, asking others to add to the story.

Then have Esau respond to Isaac, going around the room the same way. Since commentaries usually focus on how angry Esau feels toward Jacob at this point, ask Esau how he feels about his father after he has been denied the blessing. How does he feel about his mother? About his future?

✎ REFLECTIONS: ON DECEPTION

Oh, what a tangled web we weave,
When first we practice to deceive!

> —**Sir Walter Scott,** *Marmion* (1808)

Oh, what a tangled web we weave,
When first we practice to deceive!
But when we've practiced quite a while
How vastly we improve our style.

> —**J. R. Pope**

Everything that deceives may be said to enchant.

> —**Plato,** *The Republic*

He led a double life. Did that make him a liar? He did not feel a liar. He was a man of two truths.

> —**Iris Murdoch,** *The Sacred and Profane Love Machine* (1974)

When regard for truth has been broken down or even slightly weakened, all things will remain doubtful.

> —**Augustine,** *On Lying* (394 C.E.)

No legacy is so rich as honesty.

> —**William Shakespeare**, *All's Well That Ends Well*

The least initial deviation from the truth is multiplied later a thousandfold.

> —**Aristotle**, *On the Heavens*

It takes two to speak the truth—one to speak, and another to hear.

> —**Henry Thoreau**, *A Week on the Concord and Merrimack Rivers* (1849)

We are never deceived; we deceive ourselves.

> —**Johann Wolfgang von Goethe**

It is true that you may fool all the people some of the time; you can even fool some of the people all the time; but you can't fool all of the people all the time.

> —**Abraham Lincoln**, (attributed)

You can fool too many of the people too much of the time.

> —**James Thurber**, *The Thurber Carnival* (1945)

9 GOD WRESTLING

⌇ THE STORY OF JACOB'S COMING-OF-AGE: GENESIS 28, 32–33

Jacob was left alone. And a man wrestled with him until the break of dawn. (Genesis 32:25, *The Jewish Publication Society Torah*)

Anticipation and anxiety fill the air—Jacob and Esau are about to be reunited. It has been twenty years since Jacob fled his parents' house, fearing that Esau would kill him for having tricked him out of his birthright and stealing their father's blessing. The years have not been uneventful for Jacob: Leaving home, he traveled to Haran to work for his uncle Laban and, while there, married both Leah and Rachel, Laban's daughters. He became the father of eleven sons (Benjamin, the twelfth and last, was born later) and a daughter by four women—his two wives and two of their maidservants—and, eventually, became rich. When Laban's sons begin to grumble loudly about Jacob's success, however, God tells Jacob to go back to the land of his fathers and his relatives, promising that God will be with him. So Jacob packs up his wives and children, his servants and his household goods, and, twenty years after leaving, sets out for home.

Now read the story of Jacob's journey in your Bible. (If you would like to read the entire story of Jacob's journey, read Genesis 27–35.) As you do, consider the following questions:

- Who does Jacob struggle with in the night? God? An angel? Esau? Himself?

- Is there a genuine reconciliation between the brothers? Did each undergo a transformation while apart? How did each change?

- Why does Jacob encounter God at these particular moments in his life? Would any of the encounters have been possible for Jacob earlier? At what point does Jacob really seem to come of age?

- Why do Jacob's encounters with God take place at night? How does what happens at night differ in texture and quality from what happens during the daytime?

- Do you wrestle with God? With other people? With yourself?

❧ THE STRUGGLE TOWARD RECONCILIATION
by *Walter Brueggemann*

―――❧―――

Jacob is on the most dangerous mission of his life. He is about to meet his brother Esau, the one whom he had deeply wronged. Since before he was married, Jacob had done great damage to his family, and now he is on his way home, profoundly frightened—and with good reason! He has no ground for imagining that his "brother's fury" (Genesis 27:44) has been assuaged.

Jacob is a careful and prudent man. In his fearfulness, he plans and manages to prepare himself for this dangerous meeting. He uses his daytime energy to put himself in the most advantageous position he can. He sends messengers to his brother to prepare the way (32:3–5). He prays to enlist God's aid, reminding God of all promises to him still to be kept (32:9–12). He sends a series of messengers with a series of gifts to make a good appearance (32:13–20). He is utterly preoccupied and consumed with this meeting: "For he thought, I may appease him with the present that goes ahead of me, and afterwards I shall see his face; perhaps he will accept me" (32:21). While it is not evident from the translation, this single verse includes a wordplay on "face"; it is used in Hebrew five times with widely varying meanings.

But then, as happens to all of us, night comes upon Jacob and with it fatigue, exhaustion, some rest, and a great deal of restlessness. Jacob wishes for rest from his daytime work of arranging his reunion with his brother. On this night, however, he receives no rest. We are not told what kind of encounter he has—perhaps dream, perhaps nightmare. Whatever it is, it is intense, demanding, strenuous "nighttime work." Unlike his daytime work, this restless nighttime assignment is to enter into the deep unresolve that preoccupies his life. During the day, he is able to manage and take initiative. But at night, as for all of us, Jacob turns out to be vulnerable, and things rush powerfully beyond his control. His night is peopled by those uninvited and unwelcome in his life. But they are the very ones with whom he has to come to terms, if he is to go home peaceably.

This enigmatic report of his strenuous night leaves us with two great imponderables. First, it is not clear who Jacob meets in the night. That, of course, is how it is in the night. Things are unclear, and characters merge, confuse, and remain unstable. There is no doubt, on the one hand, that the character who assaults him is God. At the end, Jacob asserts, "I have seen God face to face, and yet my life is preserved" (v. 30). The wrestler has the inscrutable power of holiness hidden; he is enigmatic and elusive. On the other hand, we are told that "a man wrestled with him," i.e., a human agent, not God. When we consider who "a man" might be, the best candidate is Esau, who haunts Jacob's night as he does his day. Thus the wrestling is a "working through" of his deep anxiety about his brother.

The outcome of the wrestling is "You have striven with God and with man, and you have prevailed" (v. 28). In the daytime, we would ask, "Now which is it, God or man?" But at night things are not sorted out. There is in this meeting a convergence of the ominousness of holiness and the dreadfulness of brother. That, of course, is how it is in the night. We never get God alone, without all the complexities and unresolve of the neighborhood. And we never get wronged brother alone, without the threatening face of God. The narrator understands (as Freud belatedly understood) that the hidden powers of conflict and the hidden chance of resolve occur at night, beyond our intent. There is something of the divine in our deep human conflict and something of humanness in the holiness of God, for at night heaven and earth come at us jointly and redefine us in radical ways.

The second elusive quality in this narrative is that one cannot be sure if the "partner" in wrestling is only adversary or also advocate. The adversarial quality is unmistakable. Jacob is assaulted, evoking his deep deserved anxiety. As a consequence, he is wounded and left with a permanent visible limp. We may take this as God's judgment or as Esau's revenge. But the meeting is not all adversarial. This stranger in the night gives Jacob a new name: "Israel." Jacob finishes his night with a radically new identity, one that opens the future for his people. That ambiguous quality is how it is in the night, when we are vulnerable and not in control. In the daytime, we can distinguish between adversaries and advocates. But at night, nothing is clear, and nobody is to be trusted excessively. For the night leaves us haunted by partners who themselves give mixed and unclear messages. By engaging his anxieties, Jacob is wounded. By not flinching in the dark, he wins through to a blessing, even from an enemy who had not intended to grant a blessing.

Important things happen that night. Jacob does not overcome all of his dread, for such nighttime work is not easily transformative. He is, however, free now to meet his brother. The meeting turns out better than he anticipated: The brother he meets is more kindly disposed than the brother he had conjured. And Jacob can remember the night long enough to assert the odd mix of identities: "For truly to see your face is like seeing the face of God— since you have received me with such favor" (33:10; on "face," see 32:21).

Of course, our life of faith is like that. Biblical faith offers no God who is not embedded in the fabric of human transactions. Thus estranged brotherliness leads to estrangement from God. Reconciled brotherliness, moreover, leads to reconciliation with God.

This narrative haunts us because we are tempted to remain daytime people, knowing and in control. The story bears witness that the crucial transformations in our identity and our faith happen at night, when we are vulnerable recipients. In the darkness comes the "sibling God" who is adversary/advocate, in order to redefine us and leave us blessed and wounded, the only triumph possible in the face of God and brother.

Walter Brueggemann, a series participant, teaches Old Testament at the Columbia Theological Seminary and is the author of *The Psalms and the Life of Faith.*

ARE JACOB AND ESAU EVER REALLY RECONCILED? IS RECONCILIATION EVER POSSIBLE?

Does Jacob ever really face his brother Esau? This question itself might seem puzzling and the answer all too obvious because, after all, Genesis 33:1–17 tells the story of their encounter. But when the encounter ends and each goes his separate way once more, never to meet again except for the burial of their father Isaac (Genesis 35:29), the question lingers: Are Jacob and Esau ever really reconciled? Is reconciliation ever possible?

On the surface, things seem simple enough. First and most importantly, Esau does not kill his brother Jacob as he threatened in Genesis 27:41, thus breaking the pattern of fratricidal violence set in motion by Cain's murder of Abel in Genesis 4. Second, after observing the proprieties of polite refusal, Esau accepts Jacob's extravagant gifts, thereby restoring the material equilibrium between them that was disturbed by the loss both of his birthright (Genesis 25:29–33) and of Isaac's paternal blessing (Genesis 27). Even so, when we penetrate the veneer of Jacob's elaborate etiquette of servility, we sense that something may be amiss.

It is because Jacob is afraid to face his brother that he engages in an elaborately staged display of generosity, not because of sincere contrition or on the basis of authentic fraternal affection. In Genesis 32:21, we are offered a glimpse of Jacob's thoughts: "I will wipe (the anger from) his face with the gift that goes ahead of my face; afterward, when I see his face, perhaps he will lift up my face." With Everett Fox's rather literal version of the Hebrew text, which captures the repetition of "face" so often obscured in English translations, we begin to suspect that Jacob's gifts may be intended to insulate him from a face-to-face confrontation with Esau's wrath by their sheer quantity and to erode Esau's anger by their gradual accumulation. When Jacob exclaims, "Truly to see your face is like seeing the face of God," in the effort to convince Esau to accept his gifts, we may well wonder whether it is the terrifying aspect of the divine countenance that is subtly intended, not only the gracious face of the One Whose blessing accompanies the patriarch.

When the two men meet, Esau addresses Jacob as "my brother" throughout their encounter, yet never once does Jacob himself reciprocate in kind, preferring instead the distant and formally subservient "my lord." In the end, with Jacob's insistent refusal to allow Esau either to accompany his party or to furnish him with an escort, we are left wondering whether, deep down, anything between them has really changed. Though Jacob may have sidestepped Esau's wrath, he limps away from a missed opportunity to face Esau and see not a foe but a brother.

—**Father Jean-Pierre M. Ruiz**, a series participant, teaches at St. John's University in New York and is the editor of *The Journal of Hispanic/Latino Theology*

Jacob is a man of thought. Esau is rough, bloody, material, heedless. Jacob is all mind, Esau all animal nature.

Hence the primordial dilemma. The founding birthright/blessing is endangered: Esau, the firstborn heir, is too reckless to be worthy of the Covenant and its reciprocal obligations. He cannot hear God's charge to evolve a moral people free of idolatry—a merciful vision altogether fragile in that angry world. So Esau will be deceived, cheated of that which he would defile and destroy. His outrage confirms his unworthiness: His first impulse in feeling wronged is to murder his brother Jacob.

Jacob, who begins as an intellectual trickster, is a man of maturing imagination. Twice he is visited by dreams that purify him through God's presence. Half a lifetime afterward, punished and purged, yet still fearful of Esau's vengeance, Jacob is conciliatory and lavish with gifts. Is it the sight of all that mammoth largesse that causes the estranged Esau to run to embrace his brother? Perhaps; Jacob's humble contrition is as gratifying to long-held resentment as is a fragrant stew to the famished.

But there may be a reason more sublime: a ripened recognition in the material man that the birthright justly inheres in the man of God-dream. Esau is ready to forgive because the hard-won God-radiance in Jacob's face educates his heart. It is not enough for Esau to see that he was wronged; he must also see that he was wrong.

Self-knowledge truthfully confronted (or call it historical honesty) is the only way reconciliation can supplant murderousness. Without self-knowledge—a thing deeper than repentance—forgiveness, whether given or received, remains a hollow act.

—**Cynthia Ozick** is a novelist, essayist, and playwright. Her most recent publication is *Fame and Folly: Essays*

Sometimes peaceful coexistence is as good as reconciliation can get. We can't always become lovers or friends again after a wrong has been forgiven. I think that Esau and Jacob did about as well as they could. They ended up living amicably, if not intimately.

Which is not to be sneezed at after their fierce falling out. They were sibling rivals from before they were born, not likely to be close. But sibling rivalry is one thing: double-cross is another. And Jacob surely double-crossed Esau, cheating him out of the best thing a Hebrew older brother had going for him: his birthright. Jacob was not just incompatible with Esau; he badly injured and wronged him. No wonder Esau went after Jacob's hide.

Many years had flowed between them when the brothers met again in the desert. It looked as if Esau were still after blood; Jacob was sure he was done for. So he reverted to character and tried to buy Esau's mercy. No remorse. Not even apologies. Just bribes. So when Esau received his cheating brother with open arms, we can guess that something splendid had happened inside Esau's spirit between the time they parted and when they met again.

Esau did not need to be bought. He had forgiven Jacob. He had already cleansed his own soul of hatred. He had already surrendered his right to get even. At peace with himself (the one who does the forgiving always gets the first benefits), he was ready to be at peace with his brother.

However, their families had both gotten too big for closeness. So they settled for peaceful coexistence at a distance. As close to reconciliation as they could get. But how odd of God to let Jacob keep the blessing. Why favor Jacob, the wily, calculating cheat, over the naive, generous Esau? Who knows? Maybe it was to show that anything can happen when a God of amazing grace gets in the game.

—**Lewis B. Smedes,** a series participant, is Professor Emeritus at Fuller Theological Seminary in California, and is the author of *The Art of Forgiving*

✎ ACTIVITIES FOR GROUPS AND FAMILIES

1) GENESIS AND THE MOVIES: (UN)FORGIVEN

During the week before you meet, have different group members watch one of these films or choose a film to watch together when you meet. Forgiveness and reconciliation are central themes in *Ben-Hur* (1959), *The Chosen* (1978), *Crimes and Misdemeanors* (1989), *Death and the Maiden* (1994), *Fiddler on the Roof* (1971), *The Gathering* (1977), *In the Name of the Father* (1993), *It's a Wonderful Life* (1946), *Jean de Florette* (1986), *Manon of the Spring* (1986), *Nothing in Common* (1986), *On Golden Pond* (1981), *Ordinary People* (1980), *The Prince of Tides* (1991), *Providence* (1977), *Terms of Endearment* (1983), and *Unforgiven* (1992), among many others.

Consider: How do the characters in the films deal with injustices, past or present? Do they forgive, reconcile, exact vengeance, or do nothing? If two people reconcile in the film, what do you think made it possible? Are there things that are, in the end, simply unforgivable?

2) INTERPRETING OUR DREAMS

In most ancient cultures, dreams were considered very important. Indeed, many people, including the people who live on in the Book of Genesis, believed that God spoke to humans through their dreams.

Think about your own dreams: Do they ever have images and scenes you recognize as coming from the Bible? During the week before your meeting, write down any dreams you can remember, paying particular attention to images or symbols that could be related to the stories of Genesis or other parts of the Bible. Be creative: Try to go beyond Jacob's ladder, the serpent and the apple in the Garden, and the Ark. What about the raven and the dove with the olive branch (Noah), ascending a mountain (Abraham and Isaac), wrestling or fighting with someone (Jacob), or crossing a sea or river (Jacob going to meet Esau)? What other symbols and images can you come up with?

In talking about dreams with your group, consider: Do you believe that dreams reveal anything to us? Have you ever had a dream that you felt revealed God's plans for you? Your own plans for yourself? Have you ever had a dream that you took so seriously it changed your life, the way that Jacob's dreams did?

3) TRACKING OUR JOURNEY (PART 1): JOURNEYS OF THE SPIRIT

"Spiritual journey" may sound like New Age jargon, but the truth is that journeys of the spirit are as old as humankind—and the Bible is the repository of the accounts of some of the greatest spiritual journeys men and women have ever taken. While we may not have thought of our own lives as journeys of the spirit, we are all, to one degree or another, searching: Jacob's dark night of the soul, when he wrestles either God or a man and prevails, is not unfamiliar to us; it is a vivid dramatization of what, for most of us, happens with less fanfare, more gradually, and entirely within ourselves. To begin a discussion, have group members bring one or two objects that they feel symbolize their journeys to your next meeting and go around the circle, asking each person to tell the group about his/her objects and their significance.

⤙ REFLECTIONS: ON FORGIVENESS

And forgive us our trespasses, As we forgive those who trespass against us . . .
> —The Lord's Prayer

Forgiveness is the answer to the child's dream of a miracle by which what is broken is made whole again, what is soiled is again made clean.
> —Dag Hammarskjöld, *Markings* (1964)

He who forgives ends the quarrel.
> —African proverb

Forgiving the unrepentant is like drawing pictures on water.
> —Japanese proverb

Injuries may be forgiven but not forgotten.
> —Aesop

Forgotten is forgiven.

—F. Scott Fitzgerald

Always forgive your enemies; nothing annoys them so much.

—Oscar Wilde

Forgiveness is not an occasional act, it is a permanent attitude.

—Martin Luther King, Jr.

Without being forgiven, released from the consequences of what we could have done, our capacity to act would, as it were, be confined to one single deed from which we could never recover; we would remain victims of its consequences forever, not unlike the sorcerer's apprentice who lacked the magic formula to break the spell.

—Hannah Arendt, *The Human Condition* (1958)

Learning to forgive is much more useful than merely picking up a stone and throwing it at the object of one's anger; the more so when the provocation is extreme. For it is under the greatest adversity that there exists the greatest potential for doing good, both for oneself and others.

—Dalai Lama, *Freedom in Exile: The Autobiography of the Dalai Lama* (1990)

Bien sûr, il me pardonnera; c'est son métier. (Of course he [God] will forgive me; that's his business.)

—Heinrich Heine, last words (1856)

Once a woman has forgiven her man, she must not reheat his sins for breakfast.

—Marlene Dietrich

The weak can never forgive. Forgiveness is the attribute of the strong.

—Mahatma Gandhi

Only lies and evil come from letting people off.

—Iris Murdoch

He who has not forgiven an enemy has never yet tasted one of the most sublime enjoyments of life.

—**Johann Lavater**, *Aphorisms on Man* (ca. 1788)

Never apologize and never explain—it's a sign of weakness.

—**Frank S. Nugent and Laurence Stallings**,
She Wore a Yellow Ribbon (screenplay, 1949);
spoken by John Wayne

An apology is the superglue of life. It can repair just about everything.

—**Lynn Johnston**

Forgiveness is the freedom to make the wrong choices.

—**Lewis B. Smedes**

To be really sorry for one's errors is like opening the door to Heaven.

—**Hazrat Inayat Khan**

If you want to see the brave, look at those who can forgive.

—**Bhagavad Gita**

I have been all things unholy; if God can work through me, he can work through anyone.

—**St. Francis of Assisi**

It is easier to forgive an enemy than to forgive a friend.

—**William Blake**

It is more noble to forgive than to revenge an enemy.

—**Benjamin Franklin**

You must forgive those who transgress against you before you can look to forgiveness from God.

—**Talmud**

10 EXILE

🔖 THE STORY OF JOSEPH IN EGYPT: GENESIS 39–47

So it was, when Yosef came to his brothers,
that they stripped Yosef of his coat,
the ornamented coat that he had on,
and took him and cast him into the pit . . .

Meanwhile, some Midyanite men, merchants, passed by;
they hauled up Yosef from the pit
and sold Yosef to the Yishmaelites, for twenty pieces-of-
silver.
They brought Yosef to Egypt . . .

to Potifar, Pharaoh's court-official,
Chief of the (palace) Guard.

(Genesis 37:23–24, 28, 36, *The Five Books of Moses*,
translated by Everett Fox)

Over the centuries, many scholars have seen the last fourteen chapters of Genesis—the stories of Joseph, the son that Jacob "loved above all his sons"—as a "novella" that could have stood alone as its own book of the Bible. But Joseph's story is not set apart. This is the story that takes us from Genesis to Exodus, where Joseph's travails and triumphs in Egypt prove to have been only a hint of the travails and triumphs to come for the Israelites in Moses' generation.

The Exile program in the series and this chapter of the guide focus on the story of Joseph's exile in Egypt. Joseph has been sold into slavery by his jealous brothers and finds himself first a slave, then a prisoner, finally a powerful adviser to Pharaoh. Countless immigrants and exiles through the centuries have looked to these chapters in Genesis for guidance, not only about how to survive, but how, with luck, to flourish in a new land.

———————

Now read the story of Joseph in Egypt in your Bible. (If you would like to read the entire Joseph story, read Genesis 37–50.) As you do, consider the following questions:

- What are the costs of assimilation?

- Do you think that Joseph is a good example of a successful immigrant? Is he a realistic role model? How can an immigrant—"a stranger in a strange land"—both honor his past and, at the same time, begin to build a future? What, if anything, does the Joseph story teach us in this regard?

- In America, some of us are recent immigrants and exiles, but nearly all of us are the descendants of immigrants or exiles. Do you think many of us see ourselves in Joseph's story? Do you?

- What does this story say to Africans sold into slavery, the Vietnamese boat people, the Jews of Europe after the Holocaust, and others who did not choose to leave their homes? Can you imagine what it means to people when they know they *can't* go home again?

- What was the transformation in Joseph that enabled him to forgive and reconcile with his brothers? If Joseph's brothers had not turned up so propitiously, do you think Joseph would have ever gone home to see his family?

JOSEPH IN EXILE: A PERSONAL TESTIMONY
by Francisco O. García-Treto

In his essay, Francisco O. García-Treto, a Cuban-American minister and college professor, reexamines the Joseph story in light of his own experiences as an exile. The son of a family that fled Cuba, García-Treto says that over time he has come to read the Joseph story as his story.

I can think of two separate and very different stages in my own relationship to the biblical story of Joseph. When I was growing up in Havana, a Protestant in a Catholic country (my father was a Presbyterian minister), the story was one of many biblical tales which my parents and my teachers told as "our" story, part of the formative lore which any culture imparts in order to shape the character of its young. Like any other young Cuban, I grew up with the stories that taught me civic and patriotic virtue and made me a Cuban among Cubans, reading in school about Christopher Columbus or José Martí.

The Bible stories were another matter—these were always read with the implicit assumption that they were what made us different, what set us apart as evangélicos, as Protestants. Along with Daniel and others, Joseph was a virtuous young man, and the Lord was with him, and that was that. Amidst a popular culture whose best-known expressions in music and dance are pervaded by sexuality, a young evangélico was encouraged to flee from carnal temptation, as Joseph fled from Potiphar's wife. In my upbringing, popular music was suspect, dancing unthinkable (or clandestine), so that to this day I remain a nondancing Cuban, oxymoronic as that may seem. No wonder then, that as I try to recall the Joseph of my childhood, the figure that comes to mind is that of a rather prudish goody-goody, someone whom I both resembled and disliked. I suppose, the more I encountered that early Joseph, the more reasonable his brothers' drastic action of selling him into exile seemed to me.

As for many other Cubans, for me those days have not so much receded into the past as they have been left on the other side of a vast gulf called exile, wider certainly than the ninety-mile span of the Florida Straits. I came to the United States young enough to have done most of my undergraduate college education here, and after that, seminary and a doctorate. Here, I met and married my American wife, raised my children, became a college professor and a U.S. citizen, and now I have lived in San Antonio just over half my life.

The condition of exile and dispersion in which, along with countless others, I find myself, has given me a new standpoint for reading the Hebrew Bible—arguably a set of books largely written by exiles and for exiles—and in particular the story of Joseph. In his book *Santa Biblia: The Bible Through Hispanic Eyes*, Justo González, also a Cuban-American, describes the experience of Hispanic exiles in the United States:

> We have come to the center, yet we remain in the periphery. In a way, we no longer know where the center is—for that is the very nature of exile, a life in which one is forced to revolve around a center that is not one's own, and that in many ways one does not wish to own. Exile is a dislocation of the center, with all the ambiguities and ambivalence of such dislocation.

Like Jerusalem's exiles to Babylonia, like Latin America's exiles to the United States, Joseph found himself in Egypt as a result of an unwilled dislocation, ripped away from the center that had nurtured his childhood and youth, and placed (in his case as a slave) in the most marginal of positions in his new society. Two scenes in the Joseph story, the incident with Potiphar's wife and Joseph's appearance before Pharaoh, are illuminated in a special way when I come to them as an exile, as one who has come to know this society from the margin in rather than from the center out.

Potiphar's wife, no doubt herself a victim in her position, nevertheless easily resorts to stereotyping Joseph, who becomes "a Hebrew man" and "the Hebrew servant" in her outraged discourse in Genesis 39:14 and 39:17. Later in the story, Pharaoh's butler, who has forgotten Joseph after returning to the court from the jail where Joseph correctly interpreted his dream, likewise refers to him as "a Hebrew lad" (40:12). The exile is an alien, when seen from and by the new center, and exiles know how easily, as a class of aliens, they can be demonized, or relegated to oblivion, or romanticized. (Did the Egyptians have an equivalent of the "Latin lover" stereotype for Hebrews?) I was shocked, but not really surprised, to hear one of the candidates for presidential nomination not too long ago use "José" (Joseph) to name the stereotype of the "illegal alien" whom he was proposing to send back and fence out from the xenophobic utopia of his vision. The story of Joseph issues a warning—in the ease with which the strength of character, loyalty, and honesty of Joseph the human being become meaningless facing the accusation flung at "the Hebrew servant"—that one day there might indeed arise a new king over Egypt who had not known Joseph (see Exodus 1:8). Then the pernicious stereotypes would again cause oppression and pain.

Exiles, on the other hand, enjoy the problematic advantage of being bicultural, people who at the same time belong and don't belong to two different worlds. Just as I am Cuban-American, Joseph was a Hebrew-Egyptian, and by the denouement of the story he had become so successful in his adoption of his new identity that he could use it as a successful disguise to fool his own brothers. That, however, is just the surface of a much more complex cultural and intellectual phenomenon that all exiles, as hyphenated people, more or less consciously undergo. One aspect of that phenomenon is that, from the margin, one can see things that the center cannot see about itself, and this can work to the benefit of both center and margin. Joseph the slave did not have the investment in preserving his status at the court that probably prevented the Pharaoh's "establishment" dream interpreters from telling him the obvious truth. And Joseph the Hebrew, who had grown up in the "Third World" of his time rather than in prosperous Egypt, understood the urgency of the warning of the coming famine. When Joseph, therefore, says to his brothers that "it was to save life that God sent me on before you" (Genesis 45:5), he is speaking of the life of Egypt, as well as that of his own people.

To experience the challenge of this narrative, we might radically shift our point of view, as Justo González suggests:

> It is possible that those doing the interpretation . . . should read the story placing themselves, not in the sandals of Joseph, but rather in the shoes of the Pharaoh. In that case, the text no longer speaks so much about how good [people] ought to try to influence the powerful, but rather about how the powerful—particularly if they seek to do the will of God—must seek the alien, discover their gifts, and seek whatever wisdom and guidance those gifts might offer.

Joseph's story is a story of exile and alienation, of loss and deception, of oppression and of pain. It is the story of countless exiles, over many centuries and across many borders, who, like the exiles who wrote it and first treasured it, have loved it for its realistic portrayal of the dangers of their situation, but mainly for its affirmation of the hope that their pilgrimage will all somehow turn out for the best, that "it was to save life." And for them—for me—the story is also a story of survival and success, of reunion and reconciliation, in a word, of salvation. Stories such as this remind us also that "José" is a human being and not a stereotype, who, given a chance, may contribute more than we can imagine to our common good.

Francisco O. García-Treto, a series participant, teaches biblical studies at Trinity University in San Antonio, Texas. An ordained Presbyterian minister, he has contributed to *Harper's Dictionary of the Bible* and *The New Interpreter's Bible*.

DIVINE BEAUTY: THE QUR'ANIC STORY OF JOSEPH AND ZULAYKHĀ
by Seyyed Hossein Nasr

After a time, his master's wife cast her eyes upon Joseph, and said, "Lie with me." But he refused . . . (Genesis 39:7–8, Revised Standard Version)

The Book of Genesis tells us that working as head of household for Potiphar, Pharaoh's chief steward, presented Joseph with a difficult challenge: to find favor in the eyes of his master, while avoiding finding too much favor in the eyes of his master's wife. He is successful with Potiphar himself, but the wife of Potiphar—who has no name in the biblical versions of the text—is taken with Joseph's beauty and repeatedly tries to seduce him. Because Joseph steadfastly refuses, saying it would be a sin against God, Mrs. Potiphar denounces him to her husband, and Joseph is sent to prison. But even in prison, the text tells us, he wants for nothing and succeeds, because "God was with Joseph and extended kindness to him" (Genesis 39:21).

The story of Joseph and Mrs. Potiphar reads very differently in the Qur'an.

Then said the ladies in the city: The wife of the nobleman [Potiphar] is trying to seduce her own slave! He must indeed have smitten her with love. How foolish her conduct seems to

us! When she heard of their gossiping, she sent to them and
prepared for them a feast, and gave each of them a knife,
and said [to Joseph]: Now go out in front of them. And when
they saw him they praised him, and they cut their hands.
They said: God protect us! This is not mortal, this is nought
but a noble angel! (Qur'an, Surah XII, 30–32)

In this short piece, Seyyed Hossein Nasr tells us more about how this story
is treated in the Qur'an. One of the distinctive aspects of the Qur'anic story
is its focus on beauty and the relationship between divine and human
beauty. Joseph, the story tells us, possesses both . . .

"We narrate unto thee (Muhammad) the best of narratives." It is with these words that the Qur'an begins
the story of Joseph, which is in fact the longest continuous narrative in the sacred history of Islam as contained in its scripture.
The story to be sure is one of fatherly love, patience and sorrow,
of fraternal jealousy, of divine favor in bestowing knowledge of
dream interpretation upon one of the prophets. The salient elements of human existence as contained in the story of Joseph are
more or less shared by the Qur'anic and biblical narratives.

There is, however, another dimension of the Joseph story
which is emphasized in the Qur'anic version beyond the well-
known biblical account and which is concerned with beauty,
human and divine, personified in the relationship between God,
Joseph, and Potiphar's wife, Zulaykhā. Islam sees Joseph as the
epitome of beauty. As the twelfth-century Persian mystical philosopher Suhrawardī writes in his *Treatise on Love*, "Beauty had
already departed from the city of Adamic existence and returned
to its own world, waiting for the sign of a place which would be
worthy of the manifestation of its sovereignty. When there came
the turn of Joseph, it was informed and set out immediately. Love
grasped the sleeve of Sorrow and set out in pursuit of Beauty.
When Love came close, it saw that Beauty was so intermingled
with Joseph that there remained no difference between them."

Beauty, as a Divine Quality (one of God's Names in Islam being
the Beautiful, al-Jamīl) thus became manifested perfectly in Joseph. It is this beauty in its human form that caused Potiphar's

WHAT ARE THE COSTS OF ASSIMILATION? HAS MAKING IT IN AMERICA REQUIRED US TO GIVE UP OUR TRADITIONS, OUR LANGUAGE, OUR IDENTITY?

Joseph named the first born Manasseh, "For," he said, "God has made me forget all my hardship and all my father's house." (Genesis 41:51, *New Revised Standard Version*)

American society is a sort of flat, fresh-water pond which absorbs silently, without reaction, anything which is thrown into it.

—**Henry Adams**, letter to Royal Cortissoz,
September 20, 1911

The making of an American begins at the point where he himself rejects all other ties, any other history, and himself adopts the vesture of his adopted land.

—**James Baldwin**, *Notes of a Native Son* (1955)

We become not a melting pot but a beautiful mosaic. Different people, different beliefs, different yearnings, different hopes, different dreams.

—**Jimmy Carter**, speech, 1976

The real death of the United States will come when everyone is just alike.

—**Ralph Ellison**, interview, 1961

To an unrecognized extent, we're a nation of professional, religious, ethnic, and racial tribes . . . who maintain a fragile truce, easily and often broken. We had to conquer this continent—and its original tribes—in order to exploit its resources. But we were never able to conquer our atavistic hatreds, to accept our widely diverse pasts, to transcend them, to live together as a single people.

—**Paul Cowan**, *The Tribes of America* (1979)

But how does one bend toward another culture without falling over, how does one strike an elastic balance between rigidity and self-effacement? How does one stop reading the exterior signs of a foreign tribe and step into the inwardness, the viscera of their meanings? Every anthropologist understands the difficulty of such a feat; and so does every immigrant.

—**Eva Hoffman,** *Lost in Translation* (1989)

Coming to America has always been hard. Thriving in America is harder than ever. But so many things remain the same. And one of them is that the people who, generation to generation, believe America is a finished product are habitually revealed as people whose ideas would have impoverished this country beyond measure. It is foolish to forget where you came from, and that, in the case of the United States, is almost always somewhere else. The true authentic American is a pilgrim with a small "p" armed with little more than the phrase "I wish . . ."

—**Anna Quindlen,** *The New York Times*, 1991

There is no room in this country for hyphenated Americans . . . The one absolutely certain way of bringing this nation to ruin, of preventing all possibility of it continuing to be a nation at all, would be to permit it to become a tangle of squabbling nationalities.

—**Theodore Roosevelt,** speech, 1915

In God's eyes, we are all minorities.

—**Krister Stendahl**

Some Americans need hyphens in their names, because only part of them has come over; but when the whole man has come over, heart and thought and all, the hyphen drops of its own weight out of his name.

—**Woodrow Wilson,** speech, 1914

One ever feels his two-ness—an American, a Negro; two souls, two thoughts, two unreconciled strivings; two warring ideals in one dark body, whose dogged strength alone keeps it from being torn asunder.

—**W. E. B. Du Bois,** early twentieth century

We who are Indians today live in a world of confusion. This is the issue . . . We are Indians and we love the Indian ways. But to get along in this world the white man tells us we must be white men, that we cannot be what we were born to be.

> —**Ben Black Elk,** ca. 1968, quoted in *I Have Spoken:*
> *American History Through the Voices of the Indians*
> (1971)

Not all Americans' ancestors came here to escape tyranny; many were brought here in furtherance of tyranny. Not all crossed the ocean to better themselves and their families; many were forcibly carried here—their families torn apart, their social structures smashed, their languages suppressed . . .

> —**Hendrik Hertzberg and Henry Louis Gates, Jr.,**
> *The New Yorker,* 1996

I hear that melting pot stuff a lot, and all I can say is that we haven't melted.

> —**Jesse Jackson,** interview, 1969

To a considerable degree, the Jews survived as a vital group and as a pulsating culture because they changed their names, their language, their clothing, and with them some of their patterns of thought and expression. This ability to translate, to readapt and reorient themselves to new situations, while retaining a basic inner core of continuity, was largely responsible, if not for their survival, at least for their vitality.

> —**Gerson Cohen**, speech, 1966

There was hardly a generation in the Diaspora that did not consider itself the final link in Israel's chain. Each always saw before it the abyss ready to swallow it up.

> —**Simon Rawidowicz,** *Israel: The Ever-Dying People*
> *and Other Essays* (1986)

If one leaves the tight world of one's ancestors . . . what replacements are made in the building of the soul? How are the crises of life marked: birth, marriage, death? How are festivals managed? Men and women need ways of living within ethical frameworks, ways of passing on to their children their morality and their lifestyles. What do we do—we who once thought only of abandoning the ways of our parents and parents' parents and gave no heed to the necessary replacements, substitutes we would need to make— what do we, in our empty apartments, do to make furniture and fabric for ourselves?

—**Anne Roiphe**, *Generation Without Memory: A Jewish Journey in Christian America* (1981)

The ways my father and I saw life, the ways we lived our lives, were as different as our mother tongues, a gap of miscommunication and incomprehension that my mother tried to bridge with the language of experience, wisdom, compassion, and mostly well-timed silences.

—**Leslie Li**, quoted in *American Identities: Contemporary Multicultural Voices* (1994)

When I was ten, we emigrated to New York. How astonishing, a country where everyone spoke English! These people must be smarter, I thought. Maids, waiters, taxi drivers, doormen, bums on the street, garbagemen, all spoke this difficult language. It took some time before I understood that Americans were not necessarily a smarter, superior race.

—**Julia Alvarez**, *American Identities: Contemporary Multicultural Voices* (1994) wife to be smitten with the love of the prophet, a beauty to which the women of Egypt were to bear witness condoning her having fallen in love with Joseph because Divine Beauty, when perfectly manifested, cannot but melt the human heart. But Joseph did not respond to Zulaykhā's advances because his bond was with the vertical dimension of existence and, spiritually speaking, all horizontal human attraction has of necessity to remain subservient to the pull of the Divine Reality. Joseph's very beauty was to ensnare him in prison, to cause him pain and sorrow, but it was also to bring about finally his freedom and salvation of his family and people. It was the beauty of Joseph that finally turned the abode of sorrow of his father in Canaan into a domain of joy as the perfume of his shirt was to bring back Jacob's eyesight.

In reading the story of Joseph, we must always remember the liberating and salvific power of Divine Beauty, which turns the surface of the sea of the human soul into waves of ardent love that is only quenched when it remains in submission to the dictum of God and His Beauty and Love. Lest we forget every earthly beauty and every earthly love is a manifestation of its divine prototype, which, once realized, saves us from the confining limitations of our earthly existence.

––––––––––

Seyyed Hossein Nasr, a series participant, teaches Islamic studies at George Washington University and is the author of *Knowledge and the Sacred, Ideals and Realities of Islam,* and *Islamic Spirituality.*

QUESTIONS

- Seyyed Hossein Nasr tells us that Joseph possessed both divine and human beauty. What is the danger in confusing the two?

- How does a story like this one come to be read and interpreted so differently in different traditions? What other stories can you think of—from Genesis or from another source—where this has been the case?

ACTIVITIES FOR GROUPS AND FAMILIES

1) TRACKING OUR JOURNEY (PART 2): JOURNEYS TO NEW WORLDS

Tape a large map of the world up on a wall, give each group member different colored pencils, and ask people to trace the geographic journeys of their families on the map. Track the movements of as many generations as possible, in as much detail as possible. (In addition to moves from other countries to America, think about: moves from one state to another, from the cities to the suburbs, from the farms to urban areas.) Do you know why your relatives in each generation made the decision to move? Did they make the journey alone or with their families? Were they glad to be moving or were they forced to go? Were they able to maintain connections with their places of origin? How did they? Ask yourself: Would I be able to make the same kind of journeys as successfully as my grandparents and great-grandparents did? Would I be willing to? What would it take to make me undertake such a move?

2) LIVING IN THE NEW WORLD

Reread the quotes on assimilation included in the "Commentaries" pages in this chapter. Go around the room and ask each group member to talk about the quote or quotes that resonate most for him/her. As a group, which do you see as most hopeful? Which do you see as most realistic?

3) IMAGINING: MRS. POTIPHAR

Rewrite or retell the story of Joseph and the wife of Potiphar (Genesis 39:7–23) from her point of view. What does this add to your understanding of the story?

4) GENESIS AND THE MOVIES: COMING TO AMERICA

Pick one film from the list below to watch as a group or have individual group members watch different films (perhaps representing their own families' backgrounds) during the week before you meet. As you watch, ask yourself: How is the Old World portrayed? How is life for new American immigrants portrayed? Do Old World traditions survive in the New World? What kinds of conflicts arise in families? Between husbands and wives? Parents and children? What seem to be the causes of these tensions? (Think about: the reversal of roles when children quickly become more "American" than their parents; the difficulties of starting over; separation from extended families and friends; the loss of culture, community, language, status, and sense of place.) If you have relatives who were immigrants to America, ask them how well the movies reflect the reality of their experience and share what you learn with the group.

Some films you might want to consider: *Alamo Bay* (1985) about Vietnamese refugees on the Gulf Coast of Texas; *American Me* (1992) about thirty years in the life of an East Los Angeles Latino immigrant family; *An American Tail* (1986), an animated film about a mouse who escapes the pogroms in Russia and emigrates to America with his family; *Avalon* (1990) about three generations of Russian-Jewish immigrants who settled in Baltimore; *The Brothers McMullen* (1995) about three Irish-American brothers reexamining their Roman Catholic upbringing; *Cafe Romeo* (1991) about six lifelong friends, all second-generation Italian-Americans; *Come See the Paradise* (1990) about the internment of Americans of Japanese descent during World War II; *Crossing Delancey* (1988) about an Old World Jewish grandmother's attempts to make a match between her young, independent granddaughter and a street vendor in the Lower East Side of New York City; *Daughters of the Dust* (1991) about the danger of extinction by assimilation of the first African-American culture, the Gullah people of Georgia's sea islands, at the turn of the century; *Dim Sum: a little bit of heart* (1984), an independent film about the relationship of a Chinese mother and daughter living in San Francisco's Chinatown; *The Displaced Person* (1976), based on Flannery O'Connor's short story about a struggling Georgia farm widow who allows a Polish World War II refugee and his family to live and work on her land; *Ellis Island* (1984), a TV miniseries about three turn-of-the-century immigrants to the United States; *El Super* (1979) about Cuban exiles living in New York City, dreaming of their homeland and coping with a new culture; *The Emigrants* (1971) and its sequel, *The New Land* (1972), about poor farmers who leave Sweden in the mid-1800s and settle in Minnesota; *Far and Away* (1992) about Irish immigrants in the late 1800s; *Hester Street* (1975) about Jewish immigrants living on New York City's Lower East Side at the end of the nineteenth century; *His People* (1925), a silent film, shot on New York City's Lower East Side, about a Jewish immigrant family; *Household Saints* (1993) about three generations of Italian-American women living in New York City's Little Italy after World War II; *The Jazz Singer* (1927), the first talking film, about the son of an Orthodox cantor who wants to be a jazz singer; *The Joy Luck Club* (1993) about four strong Chinese women and their Chinese-American daughters; *King of the Gypsies* (1978) about the grandson of the patriarch of a Gypsy tribe who tries to escape his Gypsy heritage; *The Mambo Kings* (1992) about Cubans living in America; *Mississippi Masala* (1992) about Indian immigrants in the Deep South; *My Family/Mi Familia* (1995) about sixty years in the life of a Mexican-American family; *Roots* (1977), a TV miniseries, and its sequel, *Roots: The Next Generation* (1979), about African-American life in America—in the eighteenth and nineteenth centuries, through emancipation in the first miniseries and from 1882 through post-World War II in the second.

FINAL REFLECTIONS

The universe is made up of stories, not of atoms.

—Muriel Rukeyser

And I say to mankind, Be not curious about God.
For I, who am curious about each, am not curious about God; . . .
I hear and behold God in every object, yet understand God not in
  the least . . .

—Walt Whitman, *Song of Myself* (1855)

The heresy of one age becomes the orthodoxy of the next.

—Helen Keller, *Optimism* (1903)

It does no injury for my neighbor to say there are twenty gods, or no God.

—Thomas Jefferson

He who learns must suffer. And even in our sleep pain that cannot forget falls drop by drop upon the heart, and in our despair, against our will, comes wisdom to us by the awful grace of God.

—Aeschylus, *Agamemnon*

The "good guys" of the Scriptures are not plaster saints, all "sweetness and light"; nor are the "bad guys" monsters, but human beings shown in all their many (and sometimes contradictory) aspects.

—**Adin Steinsaltz,** *Biblical Images* (1984)

God is the ultimate limitation . . . No reason can be given for the nature of God because that nature is the ground of rationality. A clash of doctrines is not disaster—it is an opportunity.

—**Alfred North Whitehead,** *Science and the Modern World* (1925)

The vision of God is the greatest happiness to which man can attain . . . Our imprisonment in bodies of clay and water and entanglement in the things of sense constitute a veil which hides the Vision of God from us.

—**Abu-Hamid Muhammad al-Ghazali** (twelfth century)

What is not recorded is not remembered.

—**Benazir Bhutto,** *Daughter of Destiny* (1989)

Say not, when I have leisure I will study, you may not have leisure.

—**Ethics of the Fathers** (second century)

Re-vision—the act of looking back, of seeing with fresh eyes, of entering an old text from a new critical direction—is for women more than a chapter in cultural history: it is an act of survival.

—**Adrienne Rich,** *On Lies, Secrets, and Silence* (1979)

Man was made at the end of the week's work when God was tired.

—**Mark Twain**

The Bible is not an end but a beginning; a precedent, not a story. Its being embedded in particular historic situations has not deterred it from being everlasting. Nothing in it is surreptitious or trite. It is not an epic about the life of heroes but the story of every man in all climates and all ages. Its topic is the world, the whole of history . . . It continues to scatter seeds of justice and compassion, to echo God's cry to the world and to pierce man's armor of callousness.

—**Abraham Joshua Heschel**, *God in Search of Man* (1955)

The Bible isn't "just another book" with a lot of interesting information about God. It is a book in which people find God "coming alive," making his way into their hearts and demanding that they do something about him. He's not a "safe" or a "tame" God, securely lodged behind the bars of a distant heaven; he has the most annoying manner of showing up when we least want him; of confronting us in the strangest ways. And he usually turns out to be very different from the sort of God we would have invented ourselves. We have to be prepared for surprises and unexpected news.

—**Robert McAfee Brown**, *The Bible Speaks to You* (1985)

In spite of the patriarchal nature of biblical texts, I myself have no intention of giving up the biblical basis of my theology. In spite of its ancient and patriarchal world views, in spite of inconsistencies and mixed messages, the story of God's love affair with the world leads me to a vision of New Creation that impels my life.

—**Letty Russell**, editor, *Feminist Interpretations of the Bible* (1985)

[Genesis] is a story about the struggle to create a family whose members can live together and share a common destiny, a family which can be the foundation of the future nation. The threat to survival and continuity in Genesis comes not so much from without, but from within the patriarchal family. In each generation, the family is threatened by the twin dangers of conflict between members and loss of identity: either the family members remain together and threaten to destroy one another, or they separate and are in danger of being lost to the family's special mission.

—**Devorah Steinmetz**, *From Father to Son: Kinship, Conflict, and Continuity in Genesis* (1991)

SECTION III

RESOURCES

RECENT BOOKS ON GENESIS BY SERIES PARTICIPANTS AND GUIDE CONTRIBUTORS

Alter, Robert. *Genesis: A New Translation with Commentary.* New York: Norton, 1996.

————. *The World of Biblical Literature.* New York: Basic, 1992.

Armstrong, Karen. *In the Beginning: An Interpretation of the Book of Genesis.* New York: Knopf, 1996.

Boadt, Lawrence. *Reading the Old Testament: An Introduction.* Mahwah, N.J.: Paulist Press, 1985.

Brueggemann, Walter. *Genesis: A Bible Commentary for Teaching and Preaching.* Atlanta: John Knox, 1982.

————. *Old Testament Theology: Essays on Structure, Theme, and Text.* Minneapolis, Minn.: Fortress, 1992.

Cohen, Norman. *Self, Struggle, and Change: The Family Conflict Stories in Genesis and Their Healing Insights for Our Lives.* Woodstock, Vt.: Jewish Lights, 1995.

Fox, Everett. *The Five Books of Moses*, Volume I of the *Schocken Bible.* New York: Schocken, 1995.

Levenson, Jon D. *Creation and the Persistence of Evil: The Jewish Drama of Divine Omnipotence.* New York: Harper & Row, 1988; (reprint) Princeton, N.J.: Princeton University Press, 1994.

————. *The Death and Resurrection of the Beloved Son: The Transformation of Child Sacrifice in Judaism and Christianity.* New Haven, Ct.: Yale University Press, 1993.

Miles, Jack. *God: A Biography.* New York: Knopf, 1995.

Mitchell, Stephen. *Genesis: A New Translation of the Classical Biblical Stories.* New York: HarperCollins, 1996.

Nasr, Seyyed Hossein. *Islamic Spirituality: Foundation*, Volume I. London and New York: Crossroads, 1987.

————. *Islamic Spirituality: Manifestations*, Volume II. London and New York: Crossroads, 1991.

Pagels, Elaine H. *Adam, Eve, and the Serpent*. New York: Vintage, 1989.

Pitzele, Peter, *Our Fathers' Wells: A Personal Encounter with the Myths of Genesis*. San Francisco: HarperCollins, 1995.

Rosenblatt, Naomi, and Joshua Horwitz. *Wrestling with Angels: What the First Family Tells Us About Our Spiritual Identity, Sexuality, and Personal Relationships*. New York: Delacorte, 1995.

Smedes, Lewis B. *The Art of Forgiving*. New York: Ballantine, 1996.

Trible, Phyllis. *God and the Rhetoric of Sexuality*. Philadelphia: Fortress, 1978.

———. *Texts of Terror: Literary Feminist Readings of Biblical Narratives*. Philadelphia: Fortress, 1984.

Visotzky, Burton L. *The Genesis of Ethics*. New York: Crown, 1996.

———. *Reading the Book: Making the Bible a Timeless Text*. New York: Doubleday/Anchor, 1991; (reprint) New York: Schocken, 1996.

Wiesel, Elie. *Five Biblical Portraits*. South Bend, Ind.: Notre Dame Press, 1981.

———. *Messengers of God: Biblical Portraits and Legends*. New York: Summit, 1976.

———. *Sages and Dreamers: Biblical, Talmudic, and Hasidic Portraits and Legends*. New York: Simon & Schuster, 1991.

Zornberg, Avivah Gottlieb. *Genesis: The Beginning of Desire*. New York: Jewish Publication Society, 1995; (reprint) New York: Doubleday/Anchor, 1996.

INTERACTIVE MEDIA
RESOURCES

This list does not represent an endorsement of any product or site. It only represents information gathered from informal referrals and publications. We apologize in advance for any omissions or errors, and welcome your advice on any titles or sites we are missing. For more up-to-date information, go to public broadcasting's Web site (http://www.pbs.org or http://www.wnet.org), where the *Genesis* series will have a page.

CD-ROMs

A number of good CD-ROMs are available. On disk, you can get the Hebrew Bible (with as many as five different translations, Hebrew and English, word and topic searches, etc.), as well as the New Testament, concordances, maps, historical information, photographs, artwork, and more. Among the disks available: *BibleWorks* (Michael Bushell, publisher); *The Complete Multimedia Bible* (Compton's NewsMedia; 800-284-2045); *The New Family Bible* (Time Warner Interactive; 800-482-3766); *PC Study Bible Series* (many different titles; Bible Soft); *The QuickVerse Bible Reference Library* (Parsons Technology Inc.; 800-223-6925); and *Torah Educational Software* (many different titles). Other related titles include *The Soncino Midrash Rabbah* and *The Soncino Talmud* (Davka Corporation). Prices range from $25 to $300-plus.

THE INTERNET *AND* THE WORLD WIDE WEB

NEWSGROUPS

Newsgroups are public message-board systems in cyberspace. There are many different kinds of newsgroups related to Genesis. For example, there are newsgroups that focus on the Bible and

Bible research, including *Bible Research* (alt.christnet.bible), *Bible Studies* (christnet.bible), and *Bible Study* (soc.religion.christian. bible-study). There are also general religious newsgroups, such as *Christian Ministers* (alt.christnet), *Islam* (soc.religion.Islam), *Judaism* (soc.culture.jewish), *Religion* (talk.religion.misc), and *Religious Thought* (christnet.religion), as well as denominational newsgroups, including: *Baha'i* (soc.religion.bahai); *Buddhism* (talk.religion.buddhism); *Catholicism* (talk.religion.catholic); *Church of Christ* (alt.religion.christian.boston-church); *Quakers* (soc.religion.quaker); and *Unitarianism* (soc.religion.unitarian-univ).

SUBSCRIPTION MAILING LISTS

You can sign up to be on any number of mailing lists. That way, you will either receive all of the messages posted to a given newsgroup or, in other cases, a digest (sometimes daily, sometimes weekly) of the "best" of the newsgroup. Some related mailing lists include: *AIBI-L:* Discussion group on computerized analysis of biblical texts (*to subscribe*: Send an E-mail to listserv@ acadvm1.uottawa.ca with the text "subscribe AIBI-L Your Real Name"); *B-HEBREW:* Electronic conference for those involved in the scholarly study of the Hebrew Bible (*to subscribe*: Send an E-mail to majordomo@virginia.edu with the text "subscribe B-HEBREW [Biblical Hebrew Studies]"); *BIBLE:* Electronic conference for those interested in learning to study the Bible (*to subscribe*: send an E-mail to majordomo@virginia.edu with the text "subscribe BIBLE [Bible Study]"); *CONTENTS:* Forum for learning about newly published material on religious studies and related areas (*to subscribe*: send an E-mail to listserv@acadvm1. uottawa.ca with the text "subscribe CONTENTS Your Real Name"); *Jewish:* Forum for discussing Jewish topics, with an emphasis on Jewish law (Halakha) (*to subscribe*: send an E-mail to listserv@israel.nysernet.org with the text "subscribe jewish Your Real Name"); *MUSLIMS:* The Islamic information and news network (*to subscribe:* send an E-mail to listserv@psuvm.psu.edu with the text "subscribe MUSLIMS Your Real Name"); *Virtual Sermons from a Virtual Synagogue:* A set of sermons from the first on-line synagogue (*to subscribe*: send an E-mail to listserv@israel. nysernet.org with the text "subscribe shalomshul Your Real

Name"); and *WMSPRT-L:* Goddesses and the incorporation of the feminine/feminist idea in the study or worship of the divine (E-mail to listserv@ubvm.cc.buffalo.edu: "subscribe WMSPRT-L Your Real Name").

There are also a number of denominational mailing lists, including: *ANGLICAN* (E-mail to listserv@listserv.american.edu: "subscribe ANGLICAN Your Real Name"); *EOCHR-L (Eastern Orthodox Christianity)* (E-mail to listserv@qucdn.queensu.ca: "subscribe EOCHR-L Your Real Name); *JUDAISM* (Reform, Reconstructionist, Conservative) (E-mail to faigin@aerospace.aero.org: "liberal-judaism"); *MORMONS* (E-mail to lds-net-request@ andrew.cmu.edu: "LDS-Net"); *MUSLIMS* (E-mail to listserv@ psuvm.psu.edu: "subscribe MUSLIMS Your Real Name"); *QUAKER-P* (E-mail to listserv@vmd.cso.uluc.edu: "subscribe QUAKER-P Your Real Name"); *SPIRIT-L (Roman Catholic)* (E-mail to listserv@listserv.american.edu: "subscribe SPIRIT-L Your Real Name").

WEB SITES

A huge number of people and organizations have established Web pages. Among those to look at: *Ancient Palestine with Biblical Reference Page* (http://philae.sas.upenn.edu/ANEP/ANEP.html). *Bible Gateway:* A searchable Bible available in various translations, including the Revised Standard Version and the King James Version, and in several languages, including German, Swedish, Latin, and French (http://www.calvin.edu/cgi-bin/bible). *Christian Classics Ethereal Library:* Christian Classics from Augustine to Wesley, as well as a subject-author index, a recommended reading section, and a reference section with links to various Bible translations available on the Internet, sponsored by the University of Pittsburgh (http://www.cs.pitt.edu/~planting/books/). *Christian Theology Page:* Links to scholarly Christian theological resources on the net (http://apu.edu:80/~bstone/theology.html). *Facets of Religion:* Information on major faiths or movements, including Hinduism, Christianity, Judaism, Zoroastrianism, Buddhism, Islam, Sikhism, and Bah'ai (http://www.biologie. uni-freiburg.de/~amueller/religion/). *Islamic Texts and Resources Metapage:* Forum and links to a wide variety of resources on Islamic texts, thought, and practices, and sites providing Scriptures and Traditions and texts on Islamic thought (http://wings.

buffalo.edu/student-life/sa/muslim/isl/isl.html). *King James Version of the Bible:* A complete text in HTML 3.0 format (http://www/iadfw.net/webchap/kjvb/). *Pitts Theology Library (at Emory University) Home Page:* Provides pointers to Euclid, Emory's on-line catalog (http://sys1.pitts.emory.edu:80/ptl_home.html). *Vanderbilt University Divinity Library Home Page* (http://www.library.vanderbilt.edu/divinity/homelib.html). *World Religions:* Links to thousands of religion resources on the net, maintained by individuals or religious organizations (http://www.yahoo.com/Society_and_Culture/Religion/). *The World Wide Study Bible* (http://ccel.wheaton.edu:80/wwsb): This site has *Easton's Bible Dictionary and Sermons,* as well as *Vine's Expository Dictionary, Nave's Topical Bible, Strong's Concordance, Matthew Henry's Concise Commentary,* and *Torrey's New Topical Textbook,* from a site at Wheaton College; various versions of the Bible (including the *King James Version*) can be downloaded from hotlinks at this site; the authors of the site strongly recommend the On-Line Bible, which they call the "most capable program available without charge" (the On-line Bible can be found at: ftp://ccel.wheaton.edu/ Online Bible).

There are also many denominational home pages, such as *Amish* (http://www.epix.net/homepage/ Amish/amish.html); *Baptist Church* (http://www.utm.edu/martinarea/fbc/bra.html); *Buddhism* (http://www.psu.edu/jbe/about.html *or* http://www.mahidol.ac.th/budsir/budsir-main.html); *Catholicism* (http://www.cs.cmu.edu/Web/People/spok/catholic.html); *Episcopal Church and Worldwide Anglicanism* (http://infomatch.com:80/~haibeck/anglican.html); *Evangelical Lutheranism* (http://www.elca.org/); *Hinduism* (http://rbhatnagar.csm.uc.edu:8080/buddhist_info. html); *Judaism* (http://shamash.nysernet.org/trb/judaism.html); *Orthodox Christianity* (http://www.oct.org/OrthodoxPage); *Reformed Church (Christian)* (http://www/erc.msstate.edu/~barlow/reformed.html); *Religious Society of Friends (Quakers)* (http://www.quaker.org/); *Sikhs* (http://www.io.org:80/~sandeep/sikhism.htm); *Taoism* (http://www.cnu.edu/~patrick/taoism.html); and *United Methodist Church* (http://www.infonet. net/showcase/umsoure/).

FILE TRANSFER PROTOCOL (FTP) SITES

FTP is what allows you to copy files to and from remote computer terminals (often libraries or large databases). Two FTP sites to be aware of: *Full Text of the Babylonian and Jerusalem Talmuds, the Rambam's Yad Hachazakah, the Tanach, the Tosefta, and the Mishna:* A 1061K file that provides access to the full text of the basic primary sources in Judaism, searchable and can be printed or downloaded (FTP.JER1.CO.IL; *Path*: /pub/software/msdos/ torah/exer.zip); and *Torah Concordance:* Full searchable text of the Five Books of Moses (FTP.JER1.CO.IL; *Path*: /pub/software/ msdos/torah/tora.zip).

OUTREACH ASSOCIATES AT TIME OF PUBLICATION

～✵～

The following organizations are working with PBS's flagship station, WNET/New York, to organize Genesis discussions. For more information about how you can start a Genesis group, introduce the materials into an existing group, or partner with other community and religious organizations in your area, call WNET's Outreach Department at 212-560-2070 or your local public television station.

Alliance of Baptists
1328 16th Street, NW
Washington, DC 20036
T: 202-745-7609
F: 202-745-0023

American Bible Society
1865 Broadway
New York, NY 10023
T: 212-408-1200
F: 212-408-1512

Council of Jewish Federations
730 Broadway
New York, NY 10003
T: 212-475-5000 ext. 535
F: 212-529-5842

Episcopal Church Center
815 Second Avenue
New York, NY 10017
T: 212-922-5385
F: 212-490-6684

Friars of the Atonement
138 Waverly Place
New York, NY 10014-3845
T: 212-255-6731
F: 212-675-6160

Girls, Inc.
30 East 33rd Street
New York, NY 10016
T: 212-689-3700
F: 212-683-1253

Hadassah, WZOA
50 West 58th Street
New York, NY 10019
T: 212-355-7900
F: 212-303-4525

Institute of Christian and Jewish Studies
1316 Park Avenue
Baltimore, MD 21217
T: 410-523-7227
F: 410-523-0636

Institute of Jewish Religion
1 West 4th Street
New York, NY 10012
T: 212-674-5300 ext. 215
F: 212-388-1720

Jewish Chautauqua
838 Fifth Avenue, 4th Floor
New York, NY 10021-7064
T: 212-570-0707
F: 212-570-0960

Jewish Outreach Institute
33 West 42nd Street
New York, NY 10036
T: 212-642-2688
F: 212-642-1988

**Laymen's National Bible
   Association**
1865 Broadway
New York, NY 10023
T: 212-408-1228
F: 212-408-1448

**Louis Finkelstein Institute for
   Religious and Social Studies**
3080 Broadway
New York, NY 10027
T: 212-678-8020
F: 212-678-8947

**National Association of
   Diocesan Ecumenical Officers**
462 North Taylor
St. Louis, MO 63108
T: 314-531-9700
F: 314-531-2269

The National Conference
71 Fifth Avenue, Suite #1100
New York, NY 10011
T: 212-206-0006 ext. 234
F: 212-645-7546

**National Congress for Black
   Churches**
1225 I Street, NW, Suite #750
Washington, DC 20036
T: 202-371-1091
F: 202-371-0908

**National Council of Churches in
   the USA**
475 Riverside Drive, Suite #850
New York, NY 10115
T: 212-870-2511
F: 212-870-2030

National Council of La Raza
1111 19th Street, NW, Suite
   #2000
Washington, DC 20036
T: 202-785-1670

**National Council on Islamic
   Affairs**
230 East 44th Street, Suite #3F
New York, NY 10017
T: 212-972-0460
F: 212-682-1405

**National Federation of Temple
   Brotherhoods**
838 Fifth Avenue, Suite #1502
New York, NY 10021-7064
T: 212-570-0960
F: 212-570-0707

Neighborhood Bible Studies
34 Main Street
Dobbs Ferry, NY 10522
T: 914-693-3273
F: 914-693-4345

Outreach Judaism
P.O. Box 789
Monsey, NY 10952
T: 914-356-1915

Presbyterian Church, USA
100 Witherspoon Street
Louisville, KY 40202
T: 502-569-5000/5515
F: 502-569-5018

Rabbinical Assembly
3080 Broadway
New York, NY 10027
T: 212-678-8060
F: 212-749-9166

**Religious Public Relations
   Council, Inc.**
475 Riverside Drive, Suite #1948A
New York, NY 10115-0050
T: 212-870-3802
F: 212-870-2171

Shepherd Centers of America
6700 Troost Avenue, Suite #616
Kansas City, MO 64131
T: 816-523-1080
F: 816-523-5790

Study Circles Resource Center
Route 169, P.O. Box 203
Pomfret, CT 06258
T: 203-928-2616
F: 203-928-3713

**Union of American Hebrew
   Congregations**
838 Fifth Avenue
New York, NY 10021-7064
T: 212-650-4000
F: 212-650-4169

United Methodist Women
475 Riverside Drive, Suite #1504
New York, NY 10115
T: 212-870-3725
F: 212-870-3948

Women of Reform Judaism
838 Fifth Avenue
New York, NY 10021-7064
T: 212-650-4050
F: 212-650-4059

YWCA, USA
726 Broadway
New York, NY 10003
T: 212-614-2700
F: 212-677-9716

ACKNOWLEDGMENTS

We have been thinking about this guide for some time, but the actual work on it did not begin until after our television tapings for the series were complete. I have found this experience a delightful extension of the conversations we began while the cameras were rolling. Our hope now is that *Talking About Genesis: A Resource Guide* will help you to join in the conversation and to continue it.

This guide is the work of many devoted people. I am grateful for their efforts, their dedication, and their sustained belief in the value of this project.

The coeditors, Reverend Christopher M. Leighton and Sandee Brawarsky, keenly understand how the Bible can touch people's lives, hopes, and dreams. They brought together a thoroughly diverse and fascinating range of opinions, and by juxtaposing them, opened up these Genesis stories in new ways. I salute their creativity.

Chris took a leave of absence from his position as executive director of the Institute for Christian and Jewish Studies in Baltimore to devote his full and considerable energies to the project. He and the board of the Institute share a vision that people of different faiths must confront the dangerous distortions of the past to forge a more promising future. Sandee, a writer and editor long involved with the study of religious life, was a member of Rabbi Burt Visotzky's original Genesis discussion group—the inspiration for our television series—and has been part of the book process from its early stages. I appreciate her publishing know-how, her sensitivity to language, and her ability to listen to different views.

Noam Zion, master teacher of the Bible and member of the faculty of the Shalom Hartman Institute in Jerusalem, was also involved from the beginning, helping to conceive this guide and allowing us to borrow many of his innovative educational ideas. His unparalleled knowledge of the texts was invaluable.

For the activities that enhance each chapter, I am grateful to

Cindy Miller, whose thorough understanding of interactive educational programs and whose consultations with more than two dozen educators added greatly to this project.

Our team had the benefit of superb researchers, and I especially thank Steven Englund, who also contributed his writing and editing skills, and Kelly Washburn, who joined the endeavor in the early stages of the guide.

Katherine Kurs and Peter Pitzele contributed to various parts of the guide. Claire Kramer provided key administrative support. The staff and board of the Institute of Christian and Jewish Studies also provided support ranging from administrative help to research to brainstorming.

Many experts and educators gave generously of their time: Moti Bar-Or, Joanne Chafe, Gail Dorph, Maria Harris, Melila Hellner, Carol Lakey Hess, Carol Japha, Amichai Lau Lavie, Sara Lee, Peter Ochs, Peninnah Schram, Rabbi Stuart Seltzer, Devorah Steinmetz, Ilene Vogelstein, Alford Welch, James Williams, Walter Wink, Rabbi David Woznica, Rabbi Elana Zaiman, and Rabbi Joel Zaiman.

My own thinking has been challenged and ultimately deepened by the cross section of wise voices collected here, and I thank the many contributors of essays and short pieces.

At Doubleday, I'd especially like to thank Marly Rusoff, Sandee Yuen, Marysarah Quinn, Mark Hurst, and the other members of their talented team.

Neither the television series nor the book would have been possible without the staff of Public Affairs Television, particularly Judith Moyers, Judy Doctoroff, and Debbie Rubenstein. I also want to thank our production team—Catherine Tatge, Michael Epstein, Lisa Ammerman, and Eliza Starr Byard—along with Ann Mauzé and Robert Miller of WNET.

And none of this would have happened without the ongoing support of our funders:

Mutual of America Life Insurance Company
The Samuel Bronfman Foundation
The Nathan Cummings Foundation
The Laurence S. Rockefeller Fund
The Charles H. Revson Foundation
The Crown Family
The John D. and Catherine T. MacArthur Foundation

Righteous Persons Foundation
The Streisand Foundation
Joseph Meyerhoff Memorial Trusts
The North Star Fund
The Judy and Michael Steinhardt Foundation

Bill Moyers